Creative Worship

Creative Worship

Chris Bowater

Marshall Pickering

Marshall Morgan and Scott
Marshall Pickering
3 Beggarwood Lane, Basingstoke, Hants RG23 7LP, UK

Copyright © 1986 by Chris Bowater
First published in 1986 by Marshall Morgan and Scott Publications Ltd
Part of the Marshall Pickering Holdings Group
A subsidiary of the Zondervan Corporation

Bible references throughout are taken from the New International
Version.

British Library Cataloguing in Publication Data

Bowater, Chris
   Creative Worship.
   1. Worship
   I. Title
   264   BV10.2
   ISBN 0–551–01390–7

Phototypeset in Linotron Plantin
by Input Typesetting Ltd, London
Printed in Great Britain by
Anchor Brendon Ltd, Tiptree, Essex

This book is dedicated to my family . . . Lesley, Rachel, Daniel, Mark, Hannah and Sara . . . praying that God will cause us to be a 'visual aid' of His provision and blessing . . . and to the family of God here at 'New Life' in Lincoln.

Thanks to Beryl Jeffs and Carole Henderson for typing the manuscript and proof reading.

'Here I am,
Wholly available,
As for me
I will serve the Lord'

(Chris A Bowater 1981)

Chris Bowater's compositions have appeared in numerous publications including *Spirit of Praise*, vols 1 and 2 (Word UK), Spring Harvest books and Harvestime publications. He is also a regular contributor to *Redemption* magazine.

Contents

Introduction

'Not by might, nor by power but by my Spirit,
says the Lord Almighty.' (Zech. 4:6)

Methodology scares me sick. As soon as labels are
put on people and activities we suddenly become
experts at knowing the right names: words like
'restoration', 'apostle', 'body ministry' readily
spring to mind. They flow off the tongue so effort-
lessly. The problem with labels is that they don't
always represent the truth. One of the young men
in our Lincoln fellowship was addressing a congregation. While he was talking, he carefully opened
a tin of pears with a can-opener. The label declared
the contents to be luscious, fat, juicy Australian
pears. He took off the lid and began to pour into a
dish – baked beans! The salivary my glands
suddenly became disorientated.

We get obsessed with terminology. We go around
sticking labels on everything in church life. God is
not too interested in pinning badges to people:
'elder', 'deacon', 'chief musician', 'worship leader'
and so on. Our security is not in the badge we wear.
Our security is in what we are. God is concerned
with men, not methods, people, not posts.

Even when it comes to worship we fall into the
legalistic trap of trying to 'pigeonhole' everything.

When I was a little boy, I used to collect the little

books in the *I Spy* series: *I Spy . . . cars, I Spy . . . trains, I Spy . . . in the city, I Spy . . . in the country* and so on. Many of us have an 'I Spy . . .' mentality regarding praise and worship. How about it? *I Spy . . . charismatic praise and worship*; imagine – two points for seeing people lift their hands, three points for clapping, four points for knowing the latest Dave Fellingham chorus, five points for dancing and ten points for singing in tongues!

God is not so concerned with methods of worship. He is looking for worshippers. God is looking for people who have hearts that reach out to Him, lives that are open to His leading, ears that are sensitive to His voice. He is looking for children who will take time to develop a relationship with their father.

God is looking for 'doers' not 'knowers'. It's as if in John 14:15 Jesus was saying, 'If you love me, then do what I say.' An outworking of love is more important than an understanding of it.

Prejudiced opinion will always destroy. It will destroy relationships and will act like a tourniquet on the life-flow of the Spirit of God. God is bigger than our puny imagination. He is not restricted by our way of doing things.

I offer this book as an encouragement. It is not a text book, but hopefully a stimulus to worshipping creatively the God of all creation. It is written on the basis of two major observations: the dangers in charismatic worship and the essentials for 'flowing' in worship.

Four dangers in charismatic worship

1. Worship that is merely response to an atmos-

phere: 'Worship that depends on the externals for existence is not real worship at all; true worship is what you have left when the externals are taken away.' (Graham Kendrick *Worship*)

2. 'Play church' mentality: an attitude of programme filling, where there is plenty of 'form' but little 'power'.

3. Worshipping worship: into the latest songs but not taken up with God.

4. Unreality: a failure to take off the masks and be real. Worship involves the burning up of pretence.

Three essentials for 'flowing together' in worship

1. The body: Church is about people, people who are 'dwelling together in unity' (Ps. 133), who are prepared to move with God-given visions. God cannot work through rebellious unco-operative people.

2. The eyes: leadership with vision, a sense of direction, tuned in to the heart and plan of God.

3. The legs: those who help carry the vision, priests who carry the Ark, musicians and singers with a clear calling after God in their lives and hearts.

Chris A. Bowater

PART I

A Prepared And Willing People

We Are Gathering Together – Why?

Why are you here?
What have you come for?
Do you just come out of habit week by week?
You hear the songs, you sing the songs,
You're happy just to sing along –
But you go away
Just knowing the songs.
       ('Why are you here?' C. A. Bowater 1982)

Well, that's an impertinent question, isn't it? It's obvious why we gather together . . . after all . . . it's because . . . well, it's obvious! Now, when we've finished muttering and stuttering and hiding behind cliches about 'forsaking not the assembling', why do we come together for several hours each week? What are our motives?

Habit

When I was a child I was 'programmed', with the best of intentions, to going to church three, sometimes four times on a Sunday. Don't get me wrong; I hold no resentments. My father would, and still

3

could, organise the family with military precision. Our movements and our meals were governed by the clock. We'd be dressed up in our 'Sunday clothes' (which was hard for a little boy who was forever falling over, stepping in puddles and generally being normal), arrive at church early, sit inevitably in the same seats. It did occur to me, even at that uninformed age, that there was some subconscious territorial security in sitting in the same place week after week. But let's be careful we do not mock the 'family pew' concept until we examine our own habits.

The service then ran its predetermined course, not quickly enough by my reckoning, even to the extent of everyone knowing who would stand up and pray and, even more predictably, what they would pray. Rascal that I was, I would mentally give a score to these public prayers, assessing them by the responses of 'Amen!', 'Hallelujah!', 'Praise the Lord!', 'That's right, brother!' and so on. I was a spectator.

We would then rush home, rush dinner, rush back to church to go through it all again, suffering among other things from indigestion. In it all I was informed of the privilege of freedom to worship. Where, I ask myself, was the freedom in this worship? Let's not be mistaken, there was a discipline instilled for which I am most thankful. Something of the regimental approach has to be put into practice now with my own family.

The question is, how much of our Christian experience and practice is built merely on habit? I know of a church which lost half of its membership because the time of a meeting was changed from 11.00 a.m. to 10.30 a.m. Their routine was challenged and they could not cope with it. How often, too, one hears of a church's A.G.M. (annual grouse meeting) breaking up in confusion because members have reacted against some suggested structural change to the services – when the Lord's Table should be celebrated, or when to hold the prayer meeting.

So much of our experience is grounded in a form of Godliness with a disturbing lack of power. It has been said that the Holy Spirit could depart from many church services and programmes and would hardly be missed.

In Luke 2:41–50 we read the account of Mary and Joseph making their annual visit to Jerusalem for the Feast of the Passover. Jesus was twelve years of age and went with his parents 'according to the custom'. We read that on the homeward journey Mary and Joseph, thinking he was in their company, travelled on for a day. But Jesus wasn't with them. He was still in Jerusalem, at work on his heavenly Father's behalf.

How many churches have travelled on 'for a day', for weeks, months and years, assuming Jesus was still with them, ignorant of the fact that He was at work building His Church where His people would let Him?

A spirit of habit can not only dictate our attendance at church but also our manner of worship and what we expect of God. The Spirit of God is a life-giving Spirit and our gatherings together should manifest the very life of God, whether it be in celebration gatherings or house groups. Jesus indeed is 'in the midst', at the centre of a coming together of His people who let Him have His way amongst them.

The Atmosphere

Why are you here?
What have you come for?
Is this the social highlight of your week?
You love religious atmospheres,
They sometimes even move to tears,
But you go away
Just knowing tears.

('Why are you here?' C. A. Bowater 1982)

I was talking to a woman some while ago who is, to put it kindly, spasmodic in her attendance, but you wouldn't know it to see her in the meetings. 'I love it whenever I come here,' she enthused. 'I always have a good cry.' Now I can think of several things quite likely to make her cry, but were these tears of repentance, tears of joy and bliss in God? No. Doubtless she would cry at weddings, funerals, birthdays, flower shows and films like *The Sound of Music*. Tears that are not a result of a deep consciousness of God or do not result in change are, at best, self-centred.

A searching question that needs to be asked is this: how much of our praise and worship is merely a response to an emotional atmosphere? Now, don't get me wrong. I am not suggesting for one moment that our emotions are not involved in our praise and worship. Whole-hearted expression of gratitude for the goodness of God must involve our emotions. The point that I am making is that, if the measure of our expression of thanks and adoration to God is determined by the song being sung, the instruments being played, the fervour being generated, then that expression is second best.

Our praise and worship must emanate from a heart relationship, and not arise as a response to a created atmosphere, for it to be acceptable to God. When all that is peripheral is taken away, what is left is the measure of our praise and worship before the Lord.

Much time and energy has been devoted to the physical manifestation of so-called liberated worship: clapping, raising of hands, dancing, leaping, kneeling, bowing and so on. Now, I don't intend to spend the next few pages defending what I consider to be clearly defined scriptural principles. However, outside of the atmosphere of your Christian gathering, away from that very special spiritual motivation that takes place when we 'gather together unto Him', at home, in that quiet secret place, are we still as free in the raising of hands, dancing, bowing and kneeling?

When we come publicly before God, our lives and worship are valued according to how we are privately before God. If our private devotions are not real, then no amount of public display will compensate.

The warning note that I am sounding is that it is so easy to be swept along on a tide of enthusiasm, and yet in our hearts and in our living be genuinely desolate of blessing. Enthusiasm is not always blessing. It is even possible to be at a place where there is a real movement of God, but for our own lives to be way off the mark. Recently, at a conference attended by pastors and church leaders, I was approached by a fine-looking young man, a pastor of a small but growing fellowship. As a result of ministry, God had challenged him to the core. He revealed that for several months he had been living two lives: one, as husband and father and energetic pastor, the other in the grip of a passion for pornographic literature. He was apparently 'in blessing', but privately desolate, empty and at variance with God.

Going through the motions,
Acting out the part,
Just fine on the outside
But desolate at the heart.

The words still come so easily
Making the right sound,
But underneath the facade
The altar of the Lord is broken down.

('The Altar of the Lord' C. A. Bowater 1984)

So then, if it's not 'habit' or 'the atmosphere' or even the 'social highlight of the week', what must be the principal desire and motivation in our joining together week by week? It must be that we might know and see the manifested presence of the Lord in His glory!

Often our criterion is activity. Fill the programme: hymns and choruses, testimonies and times of sharing, special items and notices, manifestation of spiritual gifts . . . seemingly an endless Royal Command Performance! It occurs to me that it might be relevant to imagine Jesus, standing at the door of our congregation, seeking entry to impart what only His presence can bring, (Rev. 3:20), but we don't allow Him access or even let Him have a word in edgeways. 'We'll let you have your way,' we sing. 'Opportunity would be a fine thing,' replies God.

Sometimes, when we dare to let the Lord have His say, schedules and programmes have to be put away. 2 Chronicles 5:13,14 describes how when the glory of the Lord filled the house of God, those who were 'booked' to minister laid aside their ministry. Can you imagine it? All the work was finished. The house of the Lord was prepared. Choirs were rehearsed, trumpets were polished, 'the band' was ready (cymbals, psalteries and harps); the sermon for the grand opening had been sweated over for months, and then somebody started a chorus: 'The Lord is good and His mercy endureth forever'. It took off! The place resounded with their united thanksgiving, and God inhabited their praise. He joined them. His glory filled the house.

Be sure of this: when God really gets involved with the gathering of His people you may as well forget about Mrs Jones's solo, the youth item and the notices. The King must do what the King must do! He will move amongst the people in sovereign power, bringing salvation, healing and restoration – God in the midst of His people!

May God bring us to that condition of heart and quality of praise in which He can be enthroned.

Flowing Together

There is always going to be a fundamental problem when using words. The probability is that people will hear what they think is being said instead of what is actually being conveyed.

Many of us have failed an examination because we answered what we thought the question required. On closer scrutiny we discovered some important implication that had initially evaded our attention.

'Flowing in worship' happens to be one of the 'in' phrases in today's charismatic language: 'Are you in the flow, brother?', 'It really flowed this morning!'

What does it mean to 'flow together'? It is not saying the same things. We can say and sing all the right words, but still not 'flow together' in worship.

I have a friend who, when he says that he is 'hard-up', really means that he is going to have to withdraw some momeny from his building society account. He's down to his last £2,000. When I'm 'hard-up' it means that I am going through all the trouser and jacket pockets in my cloakroom hoping above all hope to find some loose change. The same words, 'hard-up', but very different in their implication.

Flowing together is not doing the same things.

There is a great deal of emphasis today on the physical manifestation in worship: clapping, dancing, leaping, the raising of hands – and rightly so.

The Hebrew word for 'High Praise' is *Tehillah*. It is *Tehillah* praise alone that God says He will inhabit, or within which He is enthroned. It is the powerful praise of warfare and victory (2 Chron. 20:22), it is the praise that is comely, becoming and appropriate (Ps. 33:1), it is the realm of praise where God manifests His glory and causes us to fear (Ex. 15:11). This is not gentle, casual, 'laid back' praise. The most often used Hebrew word associated with praise is *Halal*. It means 'to shine', 'to boast', 'to celebrate and commend'. The word also implies 'to sing until clamorously foolish'. Doesn't that paint some wild pictures in your imagination!

I believe that an extravagant, generous God desires and deserves both *Tehilla* and *Halal* praise, but a congregation that considers it is 'into' all the physical manifestations of praise are not necessarily 'flowing together' simply because they are doing the same things.

What is flowing together?

To 'flow together' is to 'see together'. 'Then thou shalt see, and flow together.' (Is. 60:5, A.V.)

What do you see?

What you see of Christ will determine how you worship Him. If you see Him only as the baby in Bethlehem's manger, or as the one who lived a good life, or if your vision of Jesus ends at the cross or even the empty tomb – then your worship will be determined by what you see.

In the book of Revelation, John repeatedly declares, 'and I saw . . .', and the throne of God was central to that unfurled revelation. God would have us come to an understanding of His throne, His Kingship and His Kingdom, to see Him high and lifted up. Then alone will we know an ever-growing recognition of who He is . . . and worship Him. 'Flowing' is to do with 'seeing'.

How do we see?

This level of vision is not according to natural eyesight. We see with the heart. It is when hearts are united, one in love and one in purpose, not merely in words, that truly it can be said 'we flow together'. When a congregation or fellowship moves into this realm of heart commitment, one to the other, our corporate worship will begin to 'flow'.

Can you sense the 'flow' indicated in this precious Psalm?

> How good and pleasant it is when brothers live together in unity!
> It is like precious oil poured on the head, running down on the beard, running down on Aaron's beard, down upon the collar of his robes.
> It is as if the dew of Hermon were falling on Mount Zion. For there the Lord bestows his blessing, even life for evermore. (Ps. 133 N.I.V.)

Unity at heart level creates a 'flowing together' that results in 'life for evermore'. Amen.

Relationships

If the Lord is not the builder
Then your labouring is vain,
Unless the Lord unites you.
Divided you'll remain,
And that which is divided
Against itself won't stand,
How can a righteous God ignore
No thought for His command?

The problem may be someone else,
The answer may be you,
Relationships are possible
To those who dare be true,
And truth amongst the brethren
Is an attitude of heart,
Someone, somewhere, someday,
Will pledge to make a start.

Then existing barriers,
Imagined or for real,
Can piece by piece be taken down,
Allowing God to heal
The hurts of insecurity,
The scars of battles done,
Let all things be relinquished
For the honour of the Son.

Let love be rich amongst you,
In reality and power,
Considering the time we live
Is God's selected hour,
In unity there's blessing,
There's strength in being one,
The spirit of the Lord still strives,
Beware lest He be gone!

(C. A. Bowater 1985)

Living together in unity may be good and pleasant, but my word, isn't it difficult? We sing lustily about being heirs of the Father and joint heirs with Christ; we link hands and declare that we are family, we are one. Truth is easy to sing about. Reality needs to match our confessions. Experience and expression must match our apparent enlightenment.

Praise and worship is a lifestyle. If I am at odds with anyone – wife, child, parent or fellow church member – my thanksgivings are not acceptable to God. He does not hear them. He will not receive them. 'First be reconciled to thy brother.' (Mt. 5:24).

How often, I wonder, do Christians come to the communion table, that most sacred of feasts, with bitterness and enmity towards someone else? Failing first of all to examine their own hearts before God (1 Cor. 11:28), they eat the bread and drink the wine 'not discerning the Lord's body' (1 Cor. 11:29). Small wonder then that so many individuals and churches are 'weak and sickly', 'sleepy' and approaching premature death (1 Cor. 11:30).

Some while ago I was ministering at a church in the north of England. It was a mid-week meeting and I was pleasantly surprised to see a congregation of about seventy people. The period of praise and worship seemed to be 'free'. The people certainly could not be faulted for exuberance. I began to minister on Psalm 133. There was fluency of tongue and buoyancy of spirit. Those of you that preach will know the feeling of cruising along a largely premeditated route. Then God intervened. He began to hold a conversation with me while I was still in full flow of preaching. He said, 'I've got something very specific for you to say to the people.'

'Oh yes, Lord?' I enquired in my heart, whilst my tongue was rattling on about oil flowing down Aaron's beard, 'What is it?'

'Tell them about genetic bitterness.'

I would, I concurred, if I knew what it meant. The oil by now was reaching to Aaron's garments.

Genetic bitterness, the Lord patiently explained, was that which underscored the lives of several members of my congregation which was now being deluged with the dew of Hermon. They had imbibed attitudes from parents and unwittingly become part of an ongoing murmur of dissatisfaction. Years before, at dinner tables and times of so-called 'fellowship', they had been systematically drained of trust and respect. Their own views had become coloured. They were now the perpetrators of someone else's grudges.

Before my now long-suffering congregation could receive further rhetoric on the dew upon the mountains of Zion, God said, 'Tell them!'

'But, Lord, what about the command of blessing, and life for evermore?'

'There can be no blessing if you don't shut up.' God can be blunt at times. 'Tell them, now.'

Homiletics took a discernible nose-dive. The purposes of God, however, became apparent. I gently shared with them what God had been saying to me. If God was speaking, I explained, He was doing it in order to bring them into a release from the bondage of genetic bitterness. A simple altar call saw fifteen people – mostly young, some weeping – stand before the Lord in repentance.

What we are before God is, in part, conditional on what we are with each other. As far as God is concerned, actions speak louder than words. Our actions can in reality deny our knowledge of Him. (Tit. 1:16).

I've always been a great listener. My home,

15

during childhood, was always a place of hospitality for visiting pastors, missionaries and the like. Instead of banishing me to some far-away room, father always allowed me to sit in a corner quietly. 'Listen and learn, son', was his firm but well-intended advice.

Somehow I can't help it, I listen to conversations on the train, in lifts and wherever people meet. I don't listen out of mere curiosity – it comes from a profound interest in people. They reveal so much about themselves by the way they speak. One can discern regional accents, levels of education, perhaps even social standing, but more revealing – the spirit of the person. The tongue betrays the real heart.

I am frequently concerned and distressed by the way Christians speak to each other. The Bible says that we should be involved in encouraging one another, building each other up in the faith, and yet how often does one hear derogatory and unkind speech amongst those who claim to belong to the Lord. Sarcasm destroys confidence. Sarcastic humour is often even worse. Within moments the same lips will be foremost in public prayer and praise! 'Out of the same mouth come praise and cursing. My brothers, this should not be.' (Jas. 3:10).

My praise must flow out from a lifestyle of praise. It is not something to be switched on like some spiritual Blackpool illumination. My relationship with my wife and children is fundamental to my relationship with God. It is an awesome thought to know that God refuses to accept my worship, however fervent or extravagant, unless it comes from a clean heart and a right spirit.

With a clean heart I'll praise You,
With a pure heart I'll honour You
With a right spirit within me,
I will magnify Your Name.

(C. A. Bowater 1984)

Let's get things right with each other. The responsibility is on us if we are aware of a relationship problem. Most of us know when things are wrong. It doesn't need times of heavy sharing. More often than not 'Sorry' or 'Will you forgive me' brings immediate healing. It may at times have to go deeper. A critical spirit is a sign of sin and needs repentance. Let us be a 'love in action' people, for only then can we lift our hands and voices and sing, 'I love You, Lord'.

Remember Psalm 133! Where this level of relationship exists amongst His people God commands His blessing. What a mighty seal of approval! Who knows, maybe you will be responsible for starting an epidemic of love in your church.

Father make us one,
That the world may see the Son,
Release through us
Streams of pure love,
Father, make us one.

(C. A. Bowater 1982)

Spirit and Truth

Because God is, there is worship. God is Spirit and desires spiritual worship from a spiritual people. In a sense, Jesus removed much of the need for discussion and debate about worship when He declared in John 4:24 that, 'they that worship the Father must worship Him in spirit and in truth'. The options are removed. Sure, you can choose *what* you worship: money, ambition, power and position or whatever, but when Father God is the object of devotion, adoration and reverence, we no longer choose *how* we worship Him. We must worship Him in the way He desires. Furthermore, He is looking for those who will do just that. (Jn. 4:23)

What, then, is it to worship in Spirit and in truth?

It appears that it is not related to a place or a tradition. The woman of Samaria, on recognising Jesus as out of the ordinary, 'a prophet'. (Jn. 4:19) albeit that hers was a partial revelation, immediately began to enter a Samaritan versus Jewish debate on worship: 'Our fathers . . . this mountain . . . you say . . . Jerusalem' (Jn. 4:20).

Have you noticed how people become defensive of their traditional positions when the person of Christ is under discussion? In reply to 'What do you think of Jesus?', along with hurried barrier constructions comes, 'Well, of course, we've always been Baptists . . .' or, 'You know, we like the way the Church of England do it.' Spirit and truth worship has nothing to do with the building, liturgy or lack of it. How often though, do we become astonishingly building-orientated. I've even heard someone say at a housegroup fellowship, 'It's not like being at church!' We are the Church – and God is building it. It's not made up of pews and chairs, pianos and organs, stained glass windows and pulpits, even hymn books and overhead projectors, beautiful or necessary though these can be. You and I are joined together, not merely in fellowship, but in a miraculous 'limb-ship', into the body of Christ, of which He is the head. God is seeking a flow of worship that comes from His body, each member in glorious, loving harmony with each other.

One hears these days, and maybe it has ever been so, certain people lamenting, 'It's not like it used to be'. What isn't? God? Has He changed? Maybe they have! Perhaps they are not so diligent, so fervent, so determined to worship the Lord as they once were. Perhaps their relationship with God is not what it used to be!

'They that worship the Father . . .' (Jn. 4:23). You see, the true worshippers, are those who are living in the reality of their relationship with God. It is a now relationship. I am secure in His Fatherhood but I must never become complacent in it.

A few years ago, when Hannah, one of my triplets, was approaching her first birthday, she was involved in an unfortunate accident, and broke her leg. It was on a day when I was due to travel some distance to preach at a fellowship in the north of England. My wife was distraught, the other children were naturally also distressed and I was faced with the most awful dilemma. Should I try and cancel the meeting, contact the team that was travelling with me . . . and so on. Dozens of possibilities and permutations of them crowded into my somewhat numbed mind. I took so long determining alternative decisions that I made none. Such is organised panic! My wife, Lesley, brought some semblance of direction at last, insisting, 'You must go!' (to the meeting).

Feeling humbled and deeply grateful to God for a life-partner with spiritual discernment, I sped up the A1 northward. Positively, that night, God spoke into the life of the fellowship and many came into a deeper understanding of His purposes. I motored home through the night, restricted not so much by the speed limit but by the capabilities of my old car. By pre-arrangement, on arriving at Lincoln in the early hours of the morning, I went straight to the local hospital. I entered the ward, somehow unusually conscious of the stillness. My footsteps became an intrusion into the peacefulness. I found Hannah's cot. Both legs were suspended in traction. She was awake but had not seen me approach. Kneeling beside her, God became so real to me. I was just preparing to leave, as unnoticed as I had arrived, when Hannah turned and saw me. It was as if someone had turned on the lights . . . she smiled . . . she shone . . . I wept. Hannah's voice, even at nearly one year old, had always been in the 'alto profundo' category, but the word 'Dad' was as sweet and melodious as anything I have ever heard. The fact that she had very few other words in her vocabulary seemed at that moment to be beside the point. The smile was one of recognition. There and then God dropped a pearl of a song into my heart:

Abba Father, Abba Father, my soul delights in
You,
Abba Father, Abba Father, my soul delights in
You,
Hallelujah my heart has cause to sing,
I'm a spirit-born, blood-bought, child of The King,
Abba Father, Abba Father, my soul delights in
You.

Worship must emanate from a current, ongoing, intimate relationship with God. When was the last time your spirit shone as you whispered, 'Father I love You, I worship and adore You.'?

I am reminded of the visit Jesus made to Bethany (Jn. 12). The home of Lazarus, Mary and Martha was frequently a haven of hospitality and solitude. Jesus loved these good people, and they loved Him. On this particular visit, Martha had busied herself, as usual, preparing and serving supper. Mary though, made the most significant demonstration of worship possible. She anointed the feet of Jesus with fragrant, refreshing spikenard ointment. To Mary it was the most obvious way of expressing love and gratitude to Jesus (who six days earlier had raised her brother Lazarus from the dead). Worship involved relationship, love and gratitude. It is worth commenting too, that the spikenard was costly. It was so costly it brought upon her a deluge of criticism, predictably from Judas Iscariot. There is cost in worship. Certainly there is a cost of concentration.

On discovering that the Greek word for 'worship' has its origin in the verb *proskuneo*, meaning 'to kiss towards', a whole new area of understanding was opened up to me. The word implies an act of total reverence. In the Scriptures worship is often associated with people bowing down or prostrating themselves.

Kissing requires concentration. I discovered this to my embarrassment and cost at a tender age. When I was thirteen years old I had my first girl-friend. At the end of the school day I would walk with her through the nearby park to her bus-stop. And then it happened. It was a warm summer evening. I had made up my mind. I would kiss her goodbye . . . my first kiss . . . my first love. I had rehearsed the kiss a thousand times in my imagination. Every time it had been executed in a wonder-fully sophisticated and mature way. Reality and dreams could not have been further from each other. I made the mistake of closing my eyes. After all, that's what happens on all the films. I aimed, lurched forward with lips protruding – and missed. The girl had moved, leaving me a feverish wreck of embarrassment. Kissing requires concentration.

How often does the Lord receive only half of our attention. Should I be invited one day to visit Her Majesty the Queen and be escorted into her throne room, I guarantee that I will not be at all bothered about the colour and texture of curtains and carpets, the flowers or the ornaments; my eyes will only be on the one who has graciously invited me to come before her throne. True worship is a throne ministry. Songs like 'Majesty', 'Jesus, we enthrone You', 'He is the King of Kings' freely pour from our lips but our minds are on so much more than the One who is enthroned in the midst of the praises of His people. We get taken up with all that is peripheral. Even the songs themselves, intended to be vehicles for our own worship, become intrusions. There is a very real danger of worshipping worship – the new songs, the atmosphere. We must see the Lord, upon the throne, and concentrate on Him alone.

Linked with this is the cost of our will. Praise and worship has nothing to do with our feelings. Our will, including our feelings, must be brought into subjection. Whether we feel like it or not, we will bless the Lord. Many people are governed by their feelings. Feelings must become secondary to the prime motivation of giving honour and glory to God. John the Baptist put it in another way, but he meant the same thing: 'He must increase, I must decrease.' (Jn. 3:30).

The Lord deserves and requires our worship and praise. We praise Him because He is our God and we are His people. (Ps. 95:6,7), because He is worthy, great and a King (Ps. 47:6,7), because we were created to praise the Lord (Ps. 102:18). It is a good thing to give thanks to the Lord. (Ps. 92:1–4).

When we praise God, we are saying, 'Thank you for all that you have done, are doing, and will do'. We recognise God's greatness and favour at work in all of creation. It is rather like a husband and wife thanking each other for all the things that they do for each other.

When we worship God, we are also saying, 'I love You for who You are'. A husband and wife relationship is not based on the statement 'Thank you for what you have done, are doing and will do for me', but rather, 'I love you for who you are'. In order to be able to say this, a husband and wife must know one another. In order for us truly to worship and love God, we have to move from the realm of praise, where we are loving Him for what He has done, into the place where we know Him.

Reality in Worship

Evangelical jargon has been perhaps the most destructive force in truly communicating the gospel. We fill our heads with phraseology that has very little relevance for the uninformed, uncommitted, and generally disinterested person. But such dearly held statements of faith are often fiction disguised as truth. Not that what we say is not true, but it has little foundation of truth in our experience. I'm talking about being real.

At the very least God wants us to be real with Him. Worship in truth depends on a recognition of who God is and an acknowledgement of who we are – in reality.

I wonder how many times we have cried to God in a prayer meeting, 'Lord, manifest Yourself, reveal Yourself and Your power'. An excellent, commendable prayer. But what if God actually took us at our word? Would we be able to handle a manifestation of His power? In truth, God is love. He is gracious and merciful, long suffering and kind. In truth also He is holy and righteous in all His ways. His anger and wrath are as relevant as the more attractive aspects of His character. We must not come before God wearing rose-coloured glasses, choosing not to see certain facets of His nature.

My children know that I love them. I tell them so often. They know I get pleasure from their fun and activities, and am usually patient with their child-like inconsistencies. They also know that I hate their lies and deceit and their abuse of each other. My love does not keep me silent but expresses itself in correction and, when necessary, punishment. They are getting to know me!

The more I get to know God, the more I find out about myself. My relationship with God cannot and must not be founded on self-deception.

One of the most honest prayers in the Scriptures was that of the one who cried, 'Lord, be merciful to me, a sinner'. Perhaps the most honest and relevant prayer we can pray is, 'Lord be merciful to me, a saint'. If we needed the mercy of God when we were still unforgiven, without hope, spiritually blind and deaf, how much more, if we have experienced His grace, and have been reborn by His Spirit, do we need His mercy, knowing as we do the way we talk about other members of His family; knowing the real level of our commitment to His will in our lives; knowing how much time we really spend allowing God to speak to us through His word and through prayer; and knowing how we 'roller-coast' on our way, being spiritual, as if nothing were really wrong. We really do need to cry for mercy.

I fear that, in the same way as we can be drawn into the evangelical jargon trap, knowing what to say and when to say it, so we can also drift into a worship-orientated jargon, knowing what to do and say in order to make it appear that we are 'in the Spirit'. Sooner or later jargon-based experience leaves an aching void, emptiness and disillusionment. My plea is for reality. 'Worship . . . in truth'.

> *My goal is God Himself, not joy, nor peace,*
> *Nor even blessing, but Himself, my God.*

(F. Brook)

In order to know Him we have to spend time in His presence. There is a cost of time.

Many Christians never move from praise to worship, because they love to spend time expressing their love to Him. In order to worship God, we have to have a change of lifestyle, where nothing else matters except our relationship with the Lord. Many live only in the realm of constantly saying 'thank you', and do not enter into the intimacy of 'I love you', simply because to express genuine love means a surrendering of wrong lifestyles and attitudes: 'If you love me, keep my commandments.' (Jn. 14:15)

We never hear of the 'sacrifice of worship' as there is no sacrifice involved. We are in a place where we know who God is, and the natural result is that we worship Him. The psalmist says that we should 'enter into His gates with thanksgiving and into His courts with praise' (Ps. 100:4). Worship is when we are able to go beyond the gates and courts into the holy and intimate place with our God. However, we cannot go into the holy place without going through the gate of thanksgiving and the courts of praise. Just as a husband and wife grow in their knowledge of each other, so too do we need to develop a life of worship. It doesn't just 'happen'. We must be worshippers, people who are dedicated to knowing our God, not just knowing about Him.

In a very real sense, also, there is a cost of our emotions. As a nation we seem to be wary of emotions, and this has overspilled into attitudes in the Church. The psalmist says, 'I will praise thee, O Lord, with my whole heart' (Ps. 9:1), and again, 'Praise ye the Lord. I will praise the Lord with my whole heart' (Ps. 111:1). Furthermore he speaks of 'delighting in the Lord' (Ps. 37:4), being 'glad and rejoicing' (Ps. 9:2), 'shouting for joy' (Ps. 32:11). Laughter, shouting, speaking, crying, calling and singing are just some of the whole-hearted attitudes of praise that consumed David's spirit. Not to mention clapping, lifting of hands, standing, bowing, dancing, kneeling, walking and being still. There are so many potential manifestations for a heart whose sole desire is to magnify the Lord. Whole-hearted worship must by implication involve a surrendering of that last bastion of our human defences, our emotions.

Could it in fact be pride that will not allow us to show what we really feel, for fear of what people will think? Worship should be God-ward alone. 'The fear of man brings us into bondage' (Prov. 29:28) but living in truth always brings liberty (Jn. 8:32).

I can well remember the time, several years ago, when my brother Anthony desired the baptism in the Holy Spirit. His natural temperament made him ultra-defensive where emotion was concerned. He had great difficulty expressing his feelings and, more importantly, he would not allow his emotions to be seen. He was a rational man and all things were dealt with on the basis of deduction and logic. He deduced, however, that he needed the indwelling power and presence of the Holy Spirit.

And the Holy Spirit is capable of reaching the parts that nothing or no one else can reach! Simply, and unemotionally, a friend and I prayed for Anthony. He had the wettest baptism in the Spirit that I have ever witnessed. For practically three hours he sobbed and wept, at times with astonishing force. God taught him how to cry! Now, the wells are very near the surface. Begin to mention something of the mercy and grace of God, His loving-kindness and faithfulness, and Anthony's eyes will readily fill with tears of gratitude and love. Worship cannot flow from a heart that is hard. That is why in the middle of Psalm 95, which is an exhortation to praise and worship, beginning, 'O come let us sing unto the Lord: let us make a joyful noise to the rock of our salvation,' David turns aside to bring a warning, 'Today if you will hear His voice, harden not your heart'.

This is an interesting Scripture. I had always associated it with passionate gospel sermons. It is, though, at the centre of a call to worship. Notice two things.

Today if you will hear His voice

What does the voice of God sound like to you? Do you know when He is speaking to you? When the triplets, Mark, Hannah and Sara, were very young, visitors to our home were astonished that we were capable of distinguishing one cry from the others. To them, they all sounded the same. To us who lived with them, and spent time with them, they were individuals and individually recognisable. The recognition of their voices came out of relationship. Our worship must emanate from a real relationship with God. Some years ago, I heard of a pastor who would personally interview people entering into membership in his church. He had standard questions that he would ask including, 'What does the voice of God sound like to you?' His own son was a candidate for membership. The pastor kept to his normal format. 'What does the voice of God sound like to you, son?' the pastor enquired. Without so much as a moment's hesitation he replied, 'Dad, he sounds just like you.' I like that. The voice of his heavenly Father was as real as his own Dad's. That young man had a real relationship with God.

Harden not your heart

How do hearts that once responded to the gentle stirrings of the Holy Spirit become hard? It is so easy to become complacent, thoughtless and 'laid back' in our relationship with the Lord. On the human level, when we begin to take someone for granted, the 'spark', the *joie de vivre* soon diminishes. Many a marriage has collapsed simply because thankfulness and mutual concern have been replaced with apathy. Amos warns about becoming complacent where once there was blessing (Amos 6:1). Psalm 95:2 says, 'Let us come into His presence with thanksgiving'. Where there is a spirit of gratitude there will be worship; where there is not you have hearts that have become hard.

> *Reign in me,*
> *Sovereign Lord, Reign in me.*
> *Captivate my heart*
> *Let Your Kingdom come,*
> *Establish there your throne,*

Let your will be done
Reign in me,
Sovereign Lord, reign in me.

(C. A. Bowater 1985)

PART II

Leadership

'I will Enter . . .'

How often have you heard it said at your church, 'Let us now enter into a time of praise and worship'?

That word 'enter' is the key to leading worship. It implies a 'coming from' and a 'moving into' – a journey. Failure and frustration occur when we try to rush or stumble into the presence of God.

As a leader, you can take the people only where you have already been. Your ability to 'lead worship' will be proportionate to the reality of your own worship life. If you find it impossible to 'press in' on God, really to draw close to Him, how can you expect to encourage those who are looking to you for leadership?

Priority

Before you stand in front of any group and say, 'Let us now enter . . .' be sure that you have already spent time with God.

Anyone (almost) can lead what is best described as a chorus medley . . . getting the enthusiastic whip out and driving people along at an exhausting pace. The task, however, is to lead, often enthusiastically, sometimes gently, but at all times sensitively.

What, then, is the purpose of first spending time alone with God? It is to tune one's heart and mind, through lingering in that 'secret place', with the heart and mind of God. You do, of course, realise that the Spirit of God has some real desires to fulfil at each gathering of God's people? More often than not the Spirit of God wants to move in the lives of His people but we don't give Him room to get involved; we crowd Him out with the never-ending chain of singing. Leaders must seek God as to the direction His Spirit desires to take. Can I hear someone saying, 'But I like to be led by the Spirit during the meeting . . .'? That's good, but it's better to be led by the Spirit *before* the meeting. The Holy Spirit needs to be released because we all have things in our lives that need to be resolved. As your heart is before God, He will give you direction, so that you can truly lead the people into that dimension of praise and worship that is purposeful. 2 Chronicles 5:11 speaks of the priests 'consecrating', or 'sanctifying' themselves before entering into the place of worship. Preparation invariably leads to a consciousness of the presence and often the power of God.

First Steps

Having prepared yourself before the Lord you will probably become very conscious that the people themselves are ill-prepared. Maybe they have not personally spent time with God or lived 'practising the presence of Christ'. Some have even come from alien environments and a transition period becomes necessary.

'Who may ascend the hill of the Lord? Who may stand in His holy place? He who has clean hands and a pure heart . . .' (Ps. 24:3,4). The condition of the heart is still central to the congregation's ability to enter into praise.

In Psalm 51, David clearly indicates a process of preparation before true praise can ascend to the Lord.

1. 'Create in me a pure heart . . .' (v. 10)

If our hearts condemn us, if sin is unconfessed, God not only cannot receive our offerings of praise, He cannot even hear them.

2. 'Renew a steadfast spirit within me . . .' (v. 10)

Our hearts can only be really clean before God if our spirits are right, and that means brothers and sisters in the Lord being right with each other.

'If you are offering your gift at the altar and there remember that your brother has something against you, leave the gift there in front of the altar. First go and be reconciled to your brother; then come and offer your gift.' (Mt. 5:23,24)

3. 'Restore to me the joy of your salvation' (v. 12)

Often in our praise there is much surface joy, but underneath the facades, there can lurk many desolate and discouraged hearts. Genuine praise will flow from hearts whose joy springs from an assurance of salvation and forgiveness. There can be no greater joy than that rooted in the knowledge and experience of forgiven sins. Then, and only then, could David cry, 'Open my lips, and my mouth shall declare your praise' (v. 15). When the heart is clean, the spirit is right and the joy restored, praise can flow.

The Costs

Be aware that there are costs involved in true worship. David declared, 'I will not sacrifice to the Lord my God burnt offerings that cost me nothing.' (Sam. 24:24)

I have already discussed the cost of the will, which we should use to stir ourselves to worship regardless of our feelings; the cost of time, which we need in order to let God have His way; the cost of emotions and the cost of concentration. Hearts and minds must come into subjection. 'I will sing with the spirit, and I will sing with the understanding also.' (1 Cor. 14:15)

I have laid down certain foundations, but these have practical implications for leaders:

1. Preparation of the leader's heart is necessary.
2. The leader should seek 'vision' or 'direction' for the meeting.
3. Part of the task is stirring the congregation physically, vocally, emotionally, to praise.
4. A standing congregation is more likely to find full involvement.
5. The leader needs to be relaxed.
6. Move purposefully from vigorous praise to more personalised worship: moving from the 'we' to the 'I'.
7. Have an open heart concerning the flow: do not automatically follow a line and procedure that was particularly blessed 'last time'.
8. As the worship becomes more intimate the leader will become less prominent. Mistiming a 'breaking in' at a time of intimate worship can be disastrous.
9. Realise that worship will ebb and flow: it is good to understand the variety of intensity that enhances the worship time.
10. Encourage the people to avoid 'second-hand worship': riding on someone else's experience or inspiration. The hymns and choruses are an excellent vehicle to take us into the realm of personal worship.

Sing a New Song

The Scriptures frequently implore us to 'sing a new song' to the Lord (Ps. 33:3, 40:3, 96:1, 98:1, 149:1;

Is. 42:10). Even heaven resounds with the strains of 'a new song' (Rev. 5:9, 14:3).

The Spirit of God is one that is creative and desires to create within us songs, new songs to the Lord

> *So from deep within*
> *My spirits singeth unto Thee*
>> (Keri Jone/David Matthews 1978)

– songs sung with the Spirit and also with the understanding. So in the midst of all the known songs that we sing when we enter into worship, let us be released into singing 'new songs' to the Lord, that find their birth in the reality of our relationship with Him.

Leading a Worship Service

Read 2 Chronicles 29:25–30 for an account of how to lead a worship service. The Lord is looking for worshippers (Jn. 4:23–24) who will worship Him in spirit and truth. When a body of God's people assemble to worship Him, somehow the worship needs to be guided. Hezekiah himself took the lead on that occasion. Today many people, whether they feel gifted or not, find themselves in the position of guiding someone else's worship to a place of fulfilment. It is an awesome duty. Whether it is a large convention meeting, a regular local church worship service or a home group gathering, many of the principles are the same.

A gifted worship leader is as valuable to a church as a good Bible teacher. Certain qualities are inherent in a good worship leader; others are acquired as skills by experience and a teachable spirit.

Obviously the worship leader is not acting alone and is faced with a number of influencing elements.

We are gathered together

We're together again . . . but in what condition? Varying states of readiness, willingness, spiritual and physical stamina, tradition and expectation are evident in most gatherings. Some people are there because they have to be, are told to be, some because they want to be. A hard day at the office or factory, family sickness, troublesome children, unconverted relatives all contribute to the attitudes prevalent at the start of a meeting. Recognise these factors and begin to join the hearts and minds of the people in the pursuit of praise.

The reason for gathering

The purpose and style of the meeting may dictate the intensity level of the praise and worship attempted. Is it a 'regular' or a 'special'? Your own folk or a mixed bunch? The style of meeting and reason for gathering needs to be clearly understood. I happen to believe that praise and worship must be central to all activity – prayer, Bible-study and yes, evangelism. On the day of Pentecost, when the promised Holy Spirit came upon the waiting followers of Jesus, as they 'declared the wonders of God' (Acts 2:11), 3,000 people were added to the Church. That's church growth. Imagine, 120 at the morning service and 3,120 at the evening. The manifestation of the Holy Spirit and worship are central to evangelism.

Who was it who said, 'Too much of a good thing is not good for you'? With celebration gatherings being so prominent in our Christian calendar there is a real danger of trying to cultivate a celebration type atmosphere in every meeting. I've known some house group meetings led with arm-waving exhilaration! The size of the gathering genuinely affects the style of praise and worship.

The celebration – probably 250 and upwards. This meeting will be centrally controlled with most initiative coming from the platform. Large gatherings lend themselves to prolonged periods of sung praise and worship. It can be sustained simply because of the number of people present and the size of the musical group.

The congregation – probably up to 200 or so people. The style of praise and worship can here be much more varied. Along with the singing, opportunity can be given for verbal participation – prayers, Bible readings, times of sharing and testimonies. The smaller the congregation becomes, the harder it is for singing to be prolonged or sustained. Greater variety of expression is required.

The cell – home group or house fellowship. The ideal size is twelve to fifteen people. Although some singing is desirable, more emphasis will be on verbal praises, sharing and ministering.

Leadership of Singing

Suddenly, it seems, a new breed of leadership has emerged: the worship leader. Some churches cannot handle any other concept than all leadership coming from a pastor or an elder. Gifting often does not even come into the equation. Unless there are clearly defined areas of responsibilities, confusion and disharmony can arise in a meeting. Who is leading? There are various possibilities.

1. Leadership can be left totally open. In fact, there is no leader. Everyone is a chief (as opposed to being Indians). This tends to be supported by the 'we want to be led by the Spirit' group. It sounds good, but in reality God sets up authorities in His Church. Leadership is part of His plan.

2. The meeting can be started off by one person then 'left open for God to move'. This too presents problems. Abdication of leadership, or responsibility, is hardly the language of the Kingdom of God.

3. The meeting is led by a group of musicians and singers. Now this is an attractive alternative. However the problem could be that everything then in terms of praise and worship takes on a musical bias, because most of us will operate in the realm of our preference. Also it is crucial that the meeting is not just being led by skilful musicians. The musicians and singers of David's tabernacle sang prophecies with skilled musical accompaniment. It is clear that they were trained and proficient (1 Chron. 25:7). How sad when some of today's finest Christian musicians are not motivated to serve in worship. However, if it comes to a choice between the skilled or the sensitive, the professional or the

prophetic, choose the one who has that prophetic anointing every time. If it is combined with musical skill, then there is potentially a dynamic ministry.
4. An alternative form of leadership is one that is clearly shared between two or three people. This works only where there is a good relationship already existing (competitive spirits cannot 'flow together'). It also works if there is a unity of vision and purpose in worship.

This 'team' style of leadership does have some real advantages. The meeting can flow with the anointing, and there is less personal pressure 'to get it right', knowing that one is being 'covered' by fellow leaders.
5. The final alternative is to have only, and probably always, one person leading, supported by the musicians. This provides continuity but may not provide sufficient contrast. All leaders have their own way of doing things, but when it becomes the only way, real progress and development can be stifled.

What shall we sing?

1. Mainly hymns with choruses relegated to the pre-service sing-a-long, or
2. Almost exclusively choruses with spontaneous song, or
3. Mainly choruses with frequent hymns and spontaneous song.

Suggestions 1 and 2 tend to imply exclusivity, whereas 3 provides breadth and flexibility of expression.

Hymns – Many churches are throwing out the hymn books. By doing so they are removing a heritage and wealth of experience that may never be replaced. Don't throw the baby out with the bath water. Rid yourselves of certain hymns that are conceptually and theologically questionable. 'Hold the fort, for I am coming' implies a 'hanging on' against all odds, a 'we'll soon be rescued from all this sin and strife' mentality. God doesn't want us to 'hold the fort' but to be a part of the building of His Church. We're not 'hanging on' but 'pressing on' from victory to victory. The Church of Jesus Christ is not in retreat but is reclaiming territory that our enemy has taken.

> We will reclaim the territory
> Where the enemy's been moving,
> We will fight with authority
> With the Holy Ghost and power.
> With a God like our God –
> What a God is our God!
> We cannot, we must not,
> We will now know defeat.
>
> (C. A. Bowater 1982)

'Gentle Jesus, meek and mild' has produced a meek and mild generation. The Jesus I serve is indeed gentle and meek but He is also the one in whom God has invested all authority. At His name devils fear and tremble. Rather let's confess:

> ' . . . that Jesus Christ is Lord . . .
> He's omnipotent, magnificent,
> All glorious, victorious . . .
> I confess that Jesus Christ is Lord!
>
> (C. A. Bowater 1982)

And what about, 'Prone to wander, Lord I feel it'? Such negative confession produces negative lives.

But in some of our hymnology there is a depth of truth expressed that we must never lose. 'No more veil, God bids me enter' (Frances Bevan) needs to be sung from generation to generation, as must 'My Goal is God Himself' (F. Brook), 'Love divine, all loves excelling' (Charles Wesley) – and so many more. The objective of hymns is to declare truth and doctrine, to teach and release worship. Let's not rob today's generation. Let's expose them to hymns that are foundational and fundamental to our faith.

Choruses – The abundance of choruses today is both a blessing and a possible blight. So many new songs . . . so many new books . . . how does one keep up with it all? There is a real pressure to keep up-to-date with the latest songs. A fellowship that tries to keep pace with every new song that bursts onto the scene will probably fall into one of various traps.

There is the possibility that no song will be able properly to filter through into the fabric of church life or into the depths of an individual's spirit. Many of the new songs need to be allowed time to become a part of the expression of the church. Choruses must be allowed to evolve; my experience is that the new songs are 'killed off' in two or three weeks.

There are choruses that have a very short life span – important in their time but without a timeless quality. Others, like certain hymns, need to be retained in the church's repertoire.

It's a good exercise to collate and classify the choruses, identifying themes, styles and key for example. Also establish those choruses that have some 'increase potential'. These are songs that can develop into extended periods of 'symphonic' praise. Some songs have this quality, others don't. I defy anyone to be able to make very much of, 'I will enter His gates with thanksgiving . . .' It's a great starter, and we have to begin somewhere, but it's not a spring-board into spontaneous song – it doesn't lend itself to too much variation of musical interpretation.

A suggested classification:

1. Thanksgiving/rejoicing/praise/gathering – of restricted 'increase' potential.
2. Thanksgiving/rejoicing/praise/gathering – of useful 'increase' potential.
3. Bright, exuberant praise.
4. 'Easy' praise.
5. 'Earnest' praise.
6. 'Grand' praise which also tilts towards worship.
7. 'Grand' worship – especially God-ward.
8. 'Earnest' worship – especially God-ward.
9. 'Easy' worship
10. Very basic worship – extreme simplicity.
11. Personal need/hunger/seeking/aspiration/ touch/blessing.
12. Themes – for example: relationships among saints; healing and ministry of Christ; commitment/availability; knowing Him; warfare and conflict; starting songs; going-out songs.

Always make a note of choruses which 'work' and say something no other chorus you know says.

I was recently reading an article written by Donald Gee, often called the pentecostal prince of writers. He said, back in 1929:

A fault we can quickly drop into in hymn and chorus singing is the placing of far too much emphasis upon our own experiences, feelings, desires, etc. We are apt to thus, all unconsciously it may be, sing about ourselves or to ourselves, or to one another, rather than 'to the Lord'. Singing is a perfectly legitimate expression of the sweetness of Christian emotion in the same way that honey is a real article of diet in the Promised Land: but there was to be no honey in the offering brought to the Lord (Lev. 2:11), and we must not confuse the expression of all our feelings of revival exhilaration with true worship in spirit and in truth. And in any case 'honey' is to be taken in moderation (Prov. 25:16). Too much singing of a 'sweet' type of hymn or chorus always produces spiritual nausea in the end. Real worship never tires.

That, I believe, has real application for the late 1980s.

Mention has been made of spontaneous song, often called (misguidedly) singing 'in the Spirit'. Bryn Barrett from Toowamba, Australia, in an article entitled 'Christian Worship' says:

Spiritual songs are those distinctive spontaneous outbursts of holy song. Anyone may have one. A whole company may have one. The Spirit Himself prompts it. If you want to know it in public then enjoy it in private. It has nothing to do with personal musical talent . . . there is that about spiritual song, that not even the world's best choirs can equal.

Preparation of your heart and spiritual life

A good leader will:
Have the heart and spirit of a worshipper. Most people really want to worship, but sometimes they have difficulty rising above the mundane aspects of their daily lives to see and experience God. Worship leaders shouldn't scold or rebuke the people of God: 'Come, stand to your feet. Don't you know He's the King of kings . . . He's worthy . . . What are you doing still sitting down in His presence . . .' Don't do it. Most of them are doing their best to magnify the Lord out of the revelation in their own hearts. The anointed leaders, those who are in touch and in tune with the people, who know how to exercise the prophetic gift and bring encouragement, will direct people's attention to God's greatness and goodness. They will aim to create an atmosphere that is charged with inspiration and illumination. The light and truth that comes into the midst of the assembly through prophetic men and women stirs, encourages and motivates God's people to thank and glorify Him. Then, set free and inspired, they have little difficulty lifting their voices to the Lord.

Bill Patton, in an article called 'Radical Worship' (*People of Destiny* magazine) said:

> This then is the role of worship leaders: they are to develop an environment where prophecy, praise and worship can flourish; they are to lead by example, prophesying themselves, and then to co-ordinate the blending together of musical and prophetic gifts so that God is exalted without inhibition.

Maintain freshness in spiritual life. Freshness springs from a real and relevant relationship with God, a current and consuming indwelling of the Holy Spirit, and a passion for the love of Christ 'that passes all knowledge'.

Be at one with the leadership in the church. You need their support and encouragement. The worship leader is potentially the first target. When the javelins start flying, you need to know that there are those around you who in every sense are 'with you'. Be at one in respect to relationships and vision. Psalm 133 often gets rewritten. It becomes ' . . . when brethren *dither* together.' There must be clarity and continuity of vision. Lack of direction could mean failure to reach the correct destination.

Have good communication with the musicians. You need them, so don't take them for granted. Involve them in prayer and planning. They may just have some valuable insight into worship. Listen to them. Share with them. Flow with them.

Be sensitive in 'administering' the anointing. Let any control be without conflict. Be prepared to move away from a pre-arranged plan. Persevere through times of 'hardness' but let any sustaining be without striving. The Spirit of God, more often than not, is a gentle spirit. He will not force His way through obstructions. But He will occupy that place where an opportunity has been made for Him to move.

Be sensitive towards the people. Have a servant's heart. Many may be inwardly crying, hurting and sore. Minister the grace of God, the all-sufficient grace.

> *You're crying inside, but there are no tears,*
> *You're trying to hide the deepest of fears.*

Tomorrow's a day you don't wish to face
But Jesus says, 'You will know today . . .
My Grace.'

(C. A. Bowater 1985)

Have a personal sense of vision and revelation concerning spiritual and scriptural worship. You are seeking to bring the congregation 'before His presence' (Ps. 95:2) in thanksgiving, in praise and rejoicing and in worship.
'Bring an offering and come before Him; worship the Lord in the splendour of His holiness.' (1 Chron. 16:29)

You are seeking to lead people to His footstool and worship (Ps. 132:7); the release of the ministering Spirit of Christ; to see God genuinely honoured.

Approaching the task

You are embarking on a journey – the most meaningful adventure that people can undertake. It begins with where we are at: acknowledging the condition we are in, and ends in the Holy of Holies with an encounter with God. The journey can be truly plotted in looking at the Psalms of ascent. (Ps. 120–134)

It begins, 'I call on the Lord in my distress . . .' (Ps. 120:1): the confession of a state of heart and mind.

It continues, 'I lift up my eyes to the hills . . .' (Ps. 121:1): the confession of longing for God and commitment to move towards Him.

It goes on, 'I rejoiced with those who said to me, "Let us go to the house of the Lord." ' (Ps. 122:1):

49

an expression of excitement, anticipation, a willingness to move.

Gradually, the songs became less person-centred and became more God-centred. They moved away from their own feelings to an awareness of God.

On this journey, recognise and appreciate the 'geographical features'. There are rises and falls; heights and depths; steep places and gentle undulations; shaded pastures and rocky paths. All feature in the journey. Let our times of praise and worship be free to explore all the wealth of expression available to us. There are times to linger by the still waters, and times to press on towards the heights. There will be periods of resting and moments of active pursuit.

Grasp the potential of each song that is being sung. Let it accomplish its potential. So often we give up on a song too early. Some songs need to be sung until they are more than words but become confessions of faith.

As you 'move with the Spirit', allow each 'turn' and 'ascent' to run its full course. We must learn how to press through even at times when it seems the going is hard. Learn how to 'move with the cloud'. The presence of God is an active, moving presence. The presence of the Lord will be there to heal, restore, forgive, encourage, enlighten . . . and much more.

Avoid too much talking. Once the people are truly pursuing that encounter with God let the 'voice over' involvement be minimal. The closer folks get to God the less aware they are of other people. The last thing they need is a third person 'dropping in' on their intimate moments with the Lord.

Don't tire the people with too many ascents or climaxes. There is no need to be afraid of silence. Just let God speak in His own inimitable way during those moments. He is able to do more in those few seconds than we can with any amount of words. Teach your people not to panic. Another chorus, a prayer, a Bible reading, even a prophecy may not in fact add to the reality of people's encounter with God; on the contrary, they could be major distractions.

At all times be gracious, in word and in gesture. Keep your countenance enthusiastic. Don't allow your mind to wander. Remember, you are leading.

Worshipping God brings us into one accord

This then is the ultimate motive of leading worship. True worship will bring everyone, be it a handful or several thousand, into the unity of the Spirit. This is the task.

> As we worship the Lord with many other Christians, we are brought into a unity, a oneness. Instead of concentrating on our differences, we look at Jesus and focus on Him. As we are caught up in the wonder of His person, those differences pale beside Him. It is as we look together to Jesus and worship Him that we are drawn closer to Him and to each other.
>
> (Roxanne Brantk, *Ministering to the Lord*)

We can never love Jesus too much. We can never spend too much time with Him. He is worthy to receive 'Glory and honour and power: for He has created all things, and for His pleasure they are and were created.' (Rev. 4:11)

Radical Prophetic Praise

I had a phone call recently from a young man in the south of the country, a young man probably very well known to many of you, who is at the forefront of involvement in leading worship and praise, and for about fifteen to twenty minutes he just poured out his heart to me, saying how empty and disillusioned he had become. Disillusioned, not with God, but with the level at which people were moving and operating in the realms of praise and worship. We have learned all the technology, as it were, of worship and praise. We have got all the equipment. We have learned what it is to become 'free in our worship and free in our praise'. But, as he said, underneath all that there has still been a niggling sense of disillusionment.

I don't want to write about techniques or methodology. I want to write about *radical prophetic praise and worship*. What do I mean by these phrases?

In all honesty, I am going to say a few things that maybe every one of us has felt but never dared say, because somehow it would not have sounded as if we were 'walking in faith and victory', and somehow it might have cast a cloud across our so-called spirituality. But if we are to be honest, many of us have had experiences in times of worship where we have not been fulfilled, where those moments have not been saturated with the real life of God. Oh, yes, they have been good meetings. But they have not been filled with the real life of God. They have not been filled with reality. They have not been filled with relevance. John 10:10: 'I have come that they may have life, and have it to the full.'

I went to a church in the northwest of the country and was greeted at the car park. The pastor came along and gave me one of those charismatic, bone-crushing hugs. I said, 'How are you?' I had obviously pressed the button and for the next five minutes it was, 'Oh, brother . . . Hallelujah . . . Glory to God . . . Isn't God wonderful? . . . We are walking in faith and victory . . . We are children of the Light . . .' and so on. For five minutes it was just a flow of positive proclamation. At the end of it all I took a breath and said, 'Really?' He said, 'No, not really . . . but no one has ever asked the second question.'

I desire that, in my worship and in my praise, more than anything else I am real. I want to be real with God because God is real. I don't want to do things just because it is expected of me. I have this year withdrawn myself from seventy-five per cent of travelling commitments. A lot of people haven't understood that but I know the need in my life for seeking God and for waiting on God for more from Him. And sometimes we get taken up with the whirligig of activity. We begin to operate on automatic. If one is used to working with people and leading people, we can make a meeting happen. We know how to get people on their feet, get them singing. And they can go away with the sense that they have been in a good meeting.

I am becoming more and more concerned that people don't just go away having been in a 'good meeting', but that they have come into contact with God; because then people will go away changed from having had a real encounter with Him. It's easy to become satisfied with the predictable patterns into which we begin to fall. Somebody once said that the only difference between a rut and a grave is the depth. It's easy to begin to get into ruts, into predictable patterns. It's easy to lose the desire to experience God in our corporate times, to lose that determination to excel in worship. But we must never, as the people of God, accept mediocrity. We must never settle for second best.

Psalm 103:1 says, 'Praise the Lord, O my soul; all my inmost being, praise His holy name.' We must desire that pursuit of excellence. Anything less becomes passive. Anything less becomes superficial, and is empty religion. We can even be 'into' the latest choruses – and I speak as a chorus writer – but in truth we worship them, or worship 'worship'.

The fundamental problem in the Old Testament with the people of God was that other things besides God began to raise themselves up in the estimation and the attention of the people, and they fell into the sin of idolatry. I would like to suggest that today there is idolatry in the Church. We have clothed our idols in all sorts of spiritual attire but I suggest that one of the idols can be the latest chorus, the latest song. We can even put people on to pedestals and allow them to become idols.

Outward expression must always reflect what is

our inner feeling and honest gratitude before God. Anything else does not bless God. Anything else is not blessing. Half-hearted mechanical worship is a waste of time. We might just as well close our meeting down. But contrast Psalm 28:7, 'My heart leaps for joy and I will give thanks to Him in song.'

One of our congregation leaders had the courage that we all wish we had at some time. His meeting started at 6.00 p.m. in his area. At 6.15 p.m. he sent everybody home. He said, 'People, you have not come desiring to meet with God. You have not come with that attitude of expectancy. And we are not just going to go through the motions. We are not having a meeting for the sake of having a meeting. Go home.' A week later they came back and they were ready. They desired to meet with God. They had that passion, that anticipation. Hebrews 13:15: 'Through Jesus, therefore, let us continually offer to God a sacrifice of praise – the fruit of lips that confess His name.'

Half-hearted mechanical worship doesn't please God. It leaves us unaffected and disillusioned. I believe that when we behold Him we are changed. That means that people will not be going out of our fellowships and out of our times of worship still carrying the same heaviness. Psalm 34:4,5: 'I sought the Lord and He answered me; He delivered me from all my fears. Those who look to Him are radiant, their faces are never covered with shame.' They will not be going out still gripped by the same fear, or entangled and crippled by that bitterness and cynicism. If, indeed, we behold Him we will be changed.

What is prophetic worship and prophetic praise? It is praise that is sustained, not by the effort of people, but by the reality of God's presence. I was in the Shetlands a few months ago in a meeting that started at 7.00 p.m. At 11.30 p.m. no one was moving. Come midnight they were still there, most of them on their knees or on their faces before God. Why? It wasn't because I was at the piano sustaining the thing and keeping it going. No. The presence of God was so heavy upon the meeting that praise and worship began to emanate out of that atmosphere at a level which I have never ever experienced.

We must not compromise our commitment to progress in worship. I believe that what is happening to fellowships in many places is that they have been to all the seminars, they have been to all the lectures. They have learnt a set of rules and principles which are good and which will bring a level of release. But they have been happy to stay at that measure of release. But that isn't progress in God. What happens if you 'plateau off' in God is that you run the risk of going backwards.

The purpose in God is to progress continually.

Worship is not a formality. It's not a preliminary activity to warm us up for the preaching, although some of us can remember when it used to be like that. The congregation got so exhausted that when they sat down they could do nothing but listen to the preaching. But on the contrary, worship is central to our reason for existence. Worship is not a press-button experience on a Sunday morning or on a particular meeting night. Worship is a lifestyle.

If you think that is a new principle, then listen to Horatius Bonar, the hymn writer of many years ago, declaring: 'Fill Thou my life, O Lord my God, in every part with praise.' What I am on Monday morning is as important to my worship life as what I appear to be on a Sunday morning. What I am with my wife and with my children is as fundamental to God in my worship life as how I appear before my pastors at the church. Because what I am in my home when the pastors and the elders are not there to be observing and giving marks out of ten, is what I really am.

Let me ask you a question. It's a question I have had to ask my own heart many times. How is your worship life at home? I don't mean only your prayer life. That is part of it. Or reading the word of God. That is also an important part of our spiritual lifestyle. But how is your worship life at home? Within all the dimensions that we are moving, in Holy Spirit liberty within the fellowship, I wonder how often what we do within the fellowship is a reaction to what everyone else is doing. You must ask yourself this question. Are you ready in your own times at home to get before the Lord and lift up hands before Him when there is no one else there except the Lord to see those hands lifted up? Are you as full of anticipation to lift up that voice of gladness when the only one who is listening to you is your Heavenly Father? Psalm 63:3,4: 'Because your love is better than life, my lips will glorify you. I will praise you as long as I live, and in your name I will lift up my hands.' What we are at home in our worship is what we really are in our worship; when we are out of the focus, out of the spotlight. Leaders – if you desire to lead your people into an area and a realm of worship you must be a worshipper.

Jesus said the Father was seeking those that worship Him (Jn. 4:24). That probably implies that

He is not finding them too readily. But the Father is seeking those that will worship Him in spirit and in truth. You can choose what you worship, but you cannot then, on the authority of God's word, choose how you worship.

Let me illustrate this. We can all choose what we worship in our lives. To some it may be that car parked outside which is your pride and joy, and you worship it. I kick mine. But you may worship yours. People do actually pour love and devotion, time and attention into their cars. But once you have selected your car to be the object of your worship, you actually have to follow a procedure of how you must worship it. You have to buy the magazines, you have to go to the clubs and the societies which cater for those with an interest in cars; buy in-car entertainment systems; expend much energy polishing it until it gleams. You begin to follow up the object of your worship with time and money. Luke 12:34, 'For where your treasure is, there your heart will be also.'

Maybe the object of your worship is money. You have chosen what you worship. But when you dream, you dream in pounds and dollars and money becomes a source of obsession in your life. Once you have chosen money to be the object of your worship you then have a necessary procedure to satisfy the longing of your worship. It's going to cost in time and attention, much outlay of money in order to accumulate money. The accumulation of possessions can, in itself, be a form of idolatry. And you can go on. You choose the object of your worship, but then you have to satisfy it. Mark 8:36, 'What good is it for a man to gain the whole world, yet forfeit his soul?' John 4:24, 'Jesus said, 'Those that worship the Father must worship in spirit and in truth.' Note that 'must' – there are no options. God is looking for a high level of truth in our lives – truth before Him.

A favourite theme of mine is the restoration of the tabernacle of David. Energetic pursuit of Biblical vision includes the restoration of prophetic worship. The time of restoration of the ark, temple and tabernacle was one of great spiritual development. Empty ritual gave way to new vibrant worship. There was the introduction of many and varied musical instruments (1 Chron. 15). It was a period when God's people praised with a loud voice (Ps. 98:4); they shouted (Ps. 47:1); they sang enthusiastically (Ps. 47:6); they sang with joyful noise (Ps. 63:5); and they danced (Ps. 150:4). These were the things that God was bringing into the life of the people of God.

But also the restoration was led by a prophetic people in celebration and praise to God. Praise was filled with the present word of the Spirit. It was filled with revelation; it was filled with the heart of God. The Psalms reflect the richness of their times together. In the tabernacle of David priority was given to worship and because of this God poured out His wisdom, His direction and power. He lifted the nation to heights of glory and influence and God was pleased to rule in their midst and manifest Himself and lead them from victory to victory. Doesn't that sound like the kind of church you want to belong to? Doesn't that sound like the kind of people that you long to be – those on whom God is pouring out His wisdom, direction and power; those whom God is lifting to heights of influence in society; those in whose midst God rules, manifesting Himself and leading from victory to victory?

Sadly, as time went on, musicians, singers, and prophetic ministries disappeared. Pure worship died in the hearts of all but a remnant. How sad. Why? It died because of moral and religious compromise, starting with the leaders. It is interesting that you read about the wisest man in the Bible, Solomon, and the strongest man in the Bible, Samson, and both of them began to fall from power and authority through moral decline. But God spoke again through Amos, about the fallen ruins being rebuilt (Amos 9:11–15). The prophetic ministries that flourished during David's reign were destined to emerge again with greater intensity and with more far-reaching effect. And that restoration is now happening. I believe we are living in days of restoration and that is not because 'restoration' is an 'in-word', in fact in some areas it is becoming an 'out-word'. See Psalm 132:13: Zion is no longer just a geographical position but a people found in every place who are moving into freedom in worship and praise, lifting hands, clapping, dancing and singing with a proliferation of many instruments, and a prophetic spirit once again coming upon the people.

So, why *radical* prophetic worship? I believe that 'radical' really means doing what we already believe. The emphasis so often in Scripture is, 'If you hear, do it. If you love me, do it.' (Jas. 1:22–25; Jn. 14:15) What is the problem? It is living in the light of the revelation that we say we have. We are so often full of revelation and yet a little slow on the outworking of it. Revelation, knowledge and understanding can either bring us into greater freedom and liberty or greater bondage – according to what we do with it. I believe to be radical is to do what we already believe in God and actually to put into practice what we hear from God. (Jas. 1:22–25; Mt. 7:24–27).

Prophetic worship is worship that is not predictable. I can remember meetings when you could actually tell the time of day by what was happening. You knew that when the elders came down to the front for the communion part of the service, it was twelve noon because that was the way it always was, ever shall be, world without end, amen! There was a predictability about our services. There was even a predictability when certain individuals stood up to pray. You knew what they were going to pray, you knew the phrases they were going to use. People would even stand up with a prophecy that they had given last week and the week before. There were tongues messages that seemed to happen every week, and you had heard them so many times you could give the same tongues messages.

I heard a story about a man who, week after week, stood up on a Sunday morning and prayed, 'Lord, take the cobwebs out of my life.' The first time that was prayed it was a pretty good prayer. But week after week went by and he was still praying, 'Lord, take the cobwebs out of my life.' At last the pastor could stand it no longer, and we know when pastors get to that point! This man stood up for his final time, 'Lord, take the cobwebs out of my life.' And the pastor, like a shot, stood up and said, 'Lord, kill the spider!'

There is a predictability in our worship. We say the same things. We do the same things. The Bible says, 'Without faith it is impossible to please God.' (Heb. 11:6) What is the level of faith in which we actually operate in our times of worship? We are moving always within the realms of what we know. Predictability ultimately kills.

Worship that is not Predictable

By all means plan for direction. We can come together and we can all stay there and hang around and say, 'I am waiting for the Spirit to move.' God probably says, 'I am waiting for you to move first.'

Let me tell you the way we do it in Lincoln. We meet as a team every week and we look back on the previous Sunday. You probably do it in your fellowship with your pastors. 'How did it go? Where did we want to go? Why didn't we get there?' We begin to think, and maybe John Shelbourne one of the pastoral team, will ask, 'If we could have changed anything, what would we have changed?' Should that prophecy have been allowed at that particular time in the meeting? Did we sing too much? Did we really give full opportunity for the people to worship? Many questions. Occasionally we simply say that we wouldn't have changed anything! But then we begin to project ourselves to the next Sunday morning's worship. The preachers among you quite reasonably expect, if you were asked to speak and bring the word of the Lord, to be given time to do that. You would not like a five-minute warning before the meeting of, 'Oh brother.

You are bringing the word of the Lord today.' But five minutes before meetings it is often said, 'Oh, you will lead the worship.'

I believe that God has things He wants to do in times of worship. I believe it's a relevant question to ask God, 'Lord, what is it You want to do amongst Your people during the worship time? What are the needs of Your people? What are the needs of Your Spirit amongst Your people this morning?' That is a fundamental question I ask of God. There is nothing worse than a situation where the people are needing to be stirred in God, they are needing that dimension of faith, and someone comes with a soft voice across the microphone to say, 'Let's be still in the presence of the Lord. Let's know that He is God.' You see, that person is saying the right things but at the wrong time. But it works the other way round too. There are times when the people do need to know what it is to linger in the presence of God and be still. Generally speaking we are very afraid of silence. We get the spiritual Polyfilla out and we try to block the silences and fill them up. Somebody thinks of a chorus. There are times when we don't need any more choruses. There are times when we don't need someone to stand up and pray. There are times when we don't need a 'word from the Lord'. I sometimes feel there are prophecies saying: 'Thus saith the Lord . . .' and God is shaking His head and saying, 'No, I haven't said it. Don't blame me.'

Somebody said in the office recently that the devil and hormones get blamed for everything. I reckon that the Lord gets blamed for a lot of things too for which He is not responsible. God is doing things. God is speaking. He is doing things in the depths of people's spirits and sometimes we can come in and confuse their ears, and we are filling their ears with words when God is already doing a great work. We need to allow for that time, and to ask God a fundamental question, 'Lord, what is it You need to do for Your people this morning?' And it may not be the same as last week.

What is Prophetic Worship?

Prophetic worship is worship that is fresh and new. A particular song was sung last week and in it God really moved. So what happens? The first song you sing the following week is that same song – you are going to try to recapture the blessing of last week. God says, 'No. I was in it last time but I have something different this time.' Isaiah 43:18,19 says, 'forget the former things; do not dwell on the past. See, I am doing a new thing. Now it springs up; do you not perceive it?' But we are creatures of habit who try to reproduce experiences, maybe even fabricate them! God is looking for those who will come before Him with freshness and newness, with an open heart, an open mind and an open spirit.

I just want to refer back to planning. You could hit problems if you don't plan, but you overplan at your peril. Overplanning can become a problem. In Lincoln we ask the Lord how He wants us to set sail. And we think of it in very clear terms like that – of setting sail. I don't know a great deal about sailing – yachts, boats, dinghies or anything else. But I do know that before the wind can do its job you have to put the sail up. That's fundamental, isn't it? There is that 'setting sail' at the beginning of the meeting, of saying, 'Lord, begin to blow by Your Spirit. Lord, we are going to set our hearts on this theme right now in You.' God says, 'Good. I have something I can work on here.' When the wind blows we don't struggle if He says, 'Now I want you to move in that direction.' We are free; we are flexible. I often fear that our large celebration gatherings feel as if they have to proceed at a hundred miles an hour. They don't. There is need for stillness, even in celebrations, allowing God to move us in different directions. We have this fixed idea that the celebration should operate at many decibels and at high speed. But that is not so. It is just another platform for God to move amongst us.

When I was in the Shetlands, there was a half hour of silence at about 11.00 p.m. during the meeting. It was a living silence. It was vital. And God was doing business and people were doing business with God. I must tell you what happened as a result of that because I shall remember it as long as I live. A woman, for the first time, began to sing a song to the Lord with a sweet voice. Somebody else picked up another refrain. Then somebody else – and the song of the Lord just went round the congregation until the whole congregation were involved. But there was no sense of predictability. There was no planning for that. That was the move of the Spirit of God. But we need to set sail. We need to plan but we must also provide opportunity for the Spirit of God to move.

We need to be fresh. We need to be new. We need to be fresh in our attitude, fresh in our desires before God. I am a great believer in having the right motives. It is fundamental to the outcome. I believe that one of the things that we need to stand against is lethargy, and that spirit of apathy that can so easily descend on the people of God. When this sort of tiredness comes upon them we need to minister something of the freshness of the Spirit of God.

Where does it come from? What causes apathy and where does freshness in the Spirit come from? It comes from the level of our expectation. What do you expect when you come together with your people on a Sunday morning? Well, I expect that the musicians will be playing by the time I sit down. I expect that the pastor and the elders will be there. I expect that the pastor will stand up and that he will begin to lead us. I expect that we will have a time of singing, and I expect that we will probably begin to sing in the Spirit. What you expect is what you'll probably get!

And by the way, have you noticed that when in doubt we sing in the Spirit? We have a problem there. It's almost like, 'What shall we do until it is evident what the next chorus should be? Let's sing in the Spirit. Musicians, make sure we stay in the right key. We'll keep it there until someone sings the relevant chorus to move on.' I'm not being cynical here. This is what really happens. We have entered into this, but we are actually now using something which is beautiful and we are abusing it.

I would rather there were times when we actually sing a new song to the Lord with our understanding because that is harder to do than singing in the Spirit. Sometimes to sing in the Spirit is a cop out. It is much harder to stand before the Lord and begin to sing, 'Lord, You are great. You are wonderful,' when other people around you can hear exactly what you are singing and saying. God is looking for us to sing a new song in words that can be understood. 1 Corinthians 14:15: 'I will sing with my spirit, but I will also sing with my mind.' God is looking for new songs from us. How can new songs come? They can only come out of hearts that know what it is to be continually renewed in God.

If I was doing a workshop, I would say, 'Right. We will sing a song. Then we will sing a new song to the Lord. We won't sing in the Spirit. We will all sing with the understanding. We will all magnify the Lord using words that we understand so that we are clear what we are saying to God.' Yes. There eventually comes a time when we run out of words. Mere words eventually become inadequate to express our feelings to God. Some of my readers will be married men. When you sit down and tell your wife you love her, you don't then go off into some strange sort of language when you have told her once. You say, 'I do love you. I think you're terrific. I appreciated that meal which you prepared for me tonight. I like the way you have your hair today.' There are so many ways we can express to our wives our gratitude and our love, using words they can understand. That makes sense.

Once a month I take the opportunity to sit in the congregation. I like to sit in the congregation, because you get a different perspective of what is going on around you. On one of these occasions I stood next to a woman, a single parent who was going through the mill. She had financial problems, there was sickness in the family and I just knew that she was having a hard time of things. During the time of worship I could hear this sweet little voice beside me singing, 'Lord, I do love You. Lord, I want to thank You for everything You are doing in my life. Lord, You are so kind to me.' I tell you this, it broke me. What it must have done to the heart of God I do not know. You see, something was coming out of her life that wasn't due to her circumstances, but arose from a heart-relationship with God. And because she sang with the understanding it did something for me. And I said, 'Lord, if she can sing like that, how much more can I. Lord, You are so kind to me as well.' And it released something in my spirit. You need to sing with the understanding. Though, as Keri Jones puts it in his song, there is a time when, 'From deep within the spirit sings unto God.' There comes a time when we just run out of knowing what to say, when the Spirit of God within us begins to give utterance before the throne.

But be fresh. Let's be new. Let's be creative in our expression of praise. Imagine that at 10.30 one Sunday morning I sit my wife down on the settee in our lounge and I say, 'I have something to say to you, Lesley. I love you. I appreciate you. I really think you are wonderful. Bless your heart.' Now the first time that would have happened she would smile back at me and perhaps says, 'Well, thank you very much. That's nice of you.' But then if the following Sunday morning at 10.30 I said, 'Love, it's time. I do love you. I think you're wonderful. Bless you,' there might still be a smile, and a frown. 'Thank you,' she would say, 'That's kind of you. Are you all right?' Then the following Sunday I say, 'It's time, Lesley. Sit down.' She would say,

'No, I won't.' 'What do you mean? It's the time when I say I love you, I appreciate you.' And she would say, 'Haven't you anything else to say?' Do you see what I am trying to say? Let's be creative before God. Let's be creative in our hearts before Him and begin to express our love and our gratitude. Let's be fresh. Let's be new in our worship. Let's be new in our application.

I wonder what it is in your life about which you have said to God, 'Never'. God has a habit of taking you at the points of your 'nevers' and making them challenging points in your life.

Muriel Shelbourne in physique and temperament is a total contrast to John. They are so different; it is unbelievable that the two are living in the same house. She is very small and quiet and John is the exact opposite. There was a time very recently when Muriel stood before the Lord and said, 'Lord, is there anything I have ever said "never" about to you?' 'Well,' God said, 'since you are asking, there is something.' 'What's that, Lord? I want to surrender that "never" to you.' 'Well, Muriel, you have said you can never dance before me.' 'Oh, yes.' Do you know what she did? She called Wesley, her sixteen-year-old son, and said, 'Wesley, don't laugh,' as she kicked off her shoes. 'I want you to sing a chorus and make it a quick one.' You can imagine a sixteen-year-old boy's reactions! 'Don't say anything, Wesley, and don't laugh. Sing something. Sing, "The Lord has led forth His people with joy." ' 'O.K. Mum.' So he started. She said, 'No, faster than that, Wesley.' And he began to sing. To his dismay and horror his mother started to skip around the kitchen, and at the end of it Muriel just knew in her spirit that she had been obedient before God. By the end she felt a little smug. 'Did you see that, Lord?' 'Yes. I was watching. But what about on a Sunday morning?' 'Lord, that wasn't part of the agreement. The agreement was that I was going to surrender my "never".' The Lord said, 'Yes, but that didn't cost you a great deal in the secrecy of your kitchen. Sunday morning, Muriel, in front of all the other people in the fellowship. I will be waiting.'

To Muriel's delight it was one of those quiet meetings. It was all gentle worship. 'Well, Lord. I was willing. You know I was willing. And I was ready, Lord.' The meeting came to its end and somebody stood up and said, 'I feel, before we go home, we ought to sing, "We shall go out with joy".' Muriel thought, 'Oh, no. I thought I had got away with it.' So the song started and there at the back of the church she began to skip. (Psalm 116:14: 'I will fulfil my vows to the Lord in the presence of all his people.') The Lord challenged her, 'Who told you to sit at the back? No one can see you. Get into the aisle and start going down to the front.' So she started skipping and dancing down the aisle. I will tell you what happened. There were other people in the fellowship who were using Muriel Shelbourne as an excuse for not dancing. Suddenly the excuse had been removed, and it released several other people into something new in God. It makes you wonder, doesn't it, what effect we have on people by the way we are, into what dimension of release we enter or don't enter.

But we need to be fresh. We need to be new in our worship. Have you found yourself moving into a period of worship where you just want to kneel before God? This isn't something that is manufactured in our meeting. It is just happening. There isn't someone saying, 'Let's all kneel'. It's happening because God is beginning to move us into new expressions of worship before Him. Be fresh. Be new.

A clear focus

I believe we need to be clearly focused in our worship. Let me tell you this. There are many costs involved in worship. David said he would not bring to the Lord that which cost him nothing (2 Sam. 24:24). Many of us are actually doing that week after week. We are bringing to the Lord that which costs us nothing. But one of the costs is a cost of concentration. Those of you in leadership and those of you who actually look across congregations know that there are people who are having problems with their concentration. There is a cost of bringing our concentration into subjection to the praise and worship that is in hand. You can look across and see that people's brains are locked into neutral. Sure they will be singing. They will be clapping. But you know there is nothing going on between their ears! When you are singing a song the mind can so easily be on other things – that hat, that tie, the dinner. Our minds can be going anywhere and everywhere while singing and clapping our song to the Lord.

I have five kids, a thirteen-year-old, an eleven-year-old, and six-year-old triplets. There is nothing better than that time of the day when they are all in bed – most parents will appreciate that. I love it on Saturday nights when they are in bed and I can sit on the settee drinking cocoa or whatever, with my wife, waiting for 'Match of the Day' to come on T.V. The sheer excitement of the moment even causes me to put my arms round her. With that encouragement she snuggles up. Then maybe just before the first match I give her a kiss on the cheek. She'll say, 'Either concentrate on me or on "Match of the Day".' There is a level of concentration that is required in any loving relationship. There is nothing worse, so I am told by my wife, than my kissing her with one eye closed and the other looking at the television. In all seriousness I believe there are times when God says, 'Will you give me your whole attention? Will you concentrate on me?'

How clearly focused is your worship and your praise? Do you bring that mind and that concentration into subjection and with all your heart concentrate on Him? Listen to this: It is only to the extent that you have seen the Lord that you can truly worship Him. Isaiah saw the Lord upon the throne. He was high and lifted up, and his train filled the temple. And the angels one to another cried, holy, holy, holy is the Lord. (Is. 6:1-3)

When Isaiah saw the Lord he gained a clearer perspective of himself and he also gained a clearer perspective of his generation. 'Lord, I am a man of unclean lips. I have seen You, Lord. Look at me. I have seen You, Lord. But look at the society I am living in. I have never really seen them in the light of your throne before.' Such a revelation could lead us into desperation and woes and yet more woes, and there would be some people who would enjoy that type of environment. But God didn't leave Isaiah there. God said, 'I know your problem. Here is the answer.' And He took some coals off the fire and touched his lips. To every problem God has an application and an answer. There are many people who sit in our congregations week after week in the morass of self-condemnation. They enjoy their woes, and they go out still woeful. But God's purposes are not for us to remain in that condition. God's purposes are that we see His throne and know the provision of cleansing. What happened to Isaiah? He heard in a way that he had never heard before. God said, 'Look, you are in this generation, I need a messenger. Who can I send?' So a sense of destiny came into Isaiah's life because of what he had seen. Do you have a real sense of destiny in your life? Maybe it is that you haven't yet seen the Lord. Have you heard the voice of the Lord and have you responded, 'Lord, here am I. Send me'? Do you want to know what the ultimate of truly focused worship is? It is a life that is truly focused in living for God. Paul says, 'Therefore, by the mercies of God, present your bodies as living worship.' (Rom. 12:1)

A clear direction

How many of you remember church services that were a little bit like spiritual bingo? 'What shall we sing? Number 44? We will sing Number 44, "He holds my hand, He holds my hand." Right, that was lovely. We haven't sung that for a few weeks, luv. That was great. Thanks for Number 44. What shall we sing? Number 66. That's a good one. That was my mother's favourite "From the rising of hhe Sun." ' Then we have 72, then we have 135 – so we have our spiritual bingo sessions.

We might say, 'We don't do that any more.' I know we don't. Do you know why? We've changed the game to 'Name that Tune'. How often are we halfway through a chorus before we know what it is? Before we know it we have drifted into a medley-sing-along style of worship, the only conceivable link from chorus to chorus being the key or the tempo of the song.

We need to be clearly focused in our worship and praise and particularly focused in the theme. I believe in God speaking to a group of people in what I call 'the seasons of the soul'. (cf. Eccles. 3) I believe that a church will go through a period of time when God is speaking about the same thing week after week after week. Carlos Ortez, something of a radical, actually says that no church should have in its teaching programme more than three subjects in a year because he believes time should be spent on teaching a subject and giving opportunity for development and application. When the church is living in the truth and reality of the teaching, then, and only then, is it time to move on to the next theme. Sadly, we move on before the truth of what we have heard becomes a relevant part of our daily lives.

The Spirit of God, in a season in the life of the fellowship, will be speaking on certain themes and certain subjects. The choruses that God gave to us in Lincoln started because of the desire to flow with what God was saying to us as a church at that time. We didn't just sing songs for the sake of singing songs. We wanted to sing songs that reinforced the things that the Spirit of God was bringing home to us. So if God was speaking about His Lordship, for instance, then God began to give us songs confessing His Lordship. There was a period of time when our Bible teacher, John Phillips was giving a beautiful series of teaching on the workings of the Holy Spirit, and the typology of the Holy Spirit. At the end of this series of teaching the Lord gave me a song, 'Come Holy Spirit, Come just as You will.' There were several verses each crystallising everything that John had been saying. God gave me this song and we taught it to the congregation. What was the result? They began to sing the truth that they had been learning.

Those things that we declare with the mouth, that we begin to sing, begin to speak, become a part of our lives. Such is the power of making confession. How many Scripture verses do you know simply because of the songs that are based on Scripture? God gave us songs that flowed in line with the teaching. We need to focus right into what the Spirit of God is saying at any particular time, not to go off at a tangent. That might mean that at your church God is going to raise up more and more song writers who are going to bring the people the 'now song' of the Lord, songs that are clearly 'in tune'.

Something that we are learning right now in Lincoln is that the things we sing need to be brought into the perspective of the reality of experience. That is what prophecy is all about. It is a word from the Lord that needs to be applied. It's a challenging thought, isn't it?

Was there a challenging word from God last Sunday in your church? What did God say? Can you remember? Most of us, by the time dinner is over, have actually forgotten what God said. That's incredible, isn't it? It is basically because we don't take these things to heart and see if there is need for application in our own lives. If there is a thing

God is reinforcing to us right now in Lincoln it is that of lifting his name above every other name. Recently we knew a mighty breakthrough in God. Something of heaven broke out amongst us. How did it start? It started by the fact that we declared our intent to magnify the name of the Lord above every other name.

But we didn't leave it there. We named every other name that might come against it. So we spoke out the name 'apathy' and we exalted the name of the Lord above it. We spoke out the name 'lethargy' and we exalted the name of the Lord above it. We spoke out the name 'fear' and we exalted the name of the Lord above it. We spoke out about sickness and we named cancer and we exalted the name of the Lord above it. So often we allow circumstances to dictate to and dominate our spirits. There are fears that people have in their lives that so captivate their hearts and imaginations that the fears are actually exalted in their thinking. We need to reverse that and begin to lift up His name. 'Take captive every thought to make it obedient to Christ.' (2 Cor. 10:5). God has invested in that name all authority and all power.

That Sunday morning we saw things happen in the most tremendous way. We saw people healed; others were baptised in the Holy Spirit. There were people who moved into a new dimension of release in God, and there were people saved during the Sunday morning service. That was because we exalted his name. Radical worship is doing what we actually say we believe. So many of these things I have shared about predictability, about freshness, about being focused, we believe. But we allow ourselves to get sidetracked into something else.

One Sunday night recently, in my congregation, we began to sing the song, 'Behold I am the Lord, the God of all flesh. Is there anything too hard for Me?' I stopped the meeting and asked what it was that people thought was hard, was a problem, and was difficult. 'Why not bring it into line with the one who is the God of all flesh, for whom there is nothing too hard?' I said. There were testimonies after that, where things were actually named and identified and brought into line with the God of all flesh, and God, as a result of this revelation, had his name returned to its correct perspective. Is there anything too hard for Him? This is the dimension of prophetic worship that we need to move into more and more.

I trust that I have scratched a few parts that may be itching. I trust I have prodded a few parts that may be hurting, and that maybe one or two areas of our understanding have been opened up a little bit. But you see, my heart is set on being a worshipper because that is what the Father is seeking. I want to please my Father. I want to honour Him. So the onus is on me and upon you to please the heart of the Father.

I want you to hear what God is saying and I hope that anything I mention which is mere debris will not be allowed to become cluttered in your hearts. It is possible for us all to be together, to listen to or to read the same things, but to understand and hear differing things. It is easy to jump ahead and think that things are being said that are not in reality. It's like a prayer meeting at which a Nigerian, for the first time, stood up and prayed a very halting prayer. He began, 'Lord, you are divine.' Then he just dried up. Some lovely sympathetic people began to fill that gap for him with, 'Hallelujah, Glory to God, You're wonderful, You're the sovereign Lord, You're the divine Lord, Oh, You are a great God. You are mighty.' This encouraged him and he plucked up the courage to start again. He continued, 'And, Lord, we are de branches.' So don't jump to conclusions in the little gaps inbetween.

Prophetic worship and praise is honest and sincere

God is not wanting hypocritical praise. He does not require lip service. But He does require clean hearts, right spirits and those in whom joy is restored (Ps. 51). The condition of our heart is central to the issue of praise. Pretence does not please God. Looking apparently enraptured by His presence when in reality heart and mind are wayward, distant or, at best, merely locked into neutral, does not please God.

Truth is a high priority in worship. The Father seeks truth. Far better to be honest and acknowledge that we are 'out of sorts' than to seem outwardly to be consumed with love but be inwardly condemned for hypoccrisy.

Someone once said that God is like a best friend: He doesn't mind if we're not speaking to Him as long as He doesn't find it out from someone else. Begin to express the reality of your condition. Begin to state an intention to worship. My experience is that in giving praise and honour, a positive act of giving, something is renewed and rekindled in the depths of our spirits.

Prophetic praise is responsive

Those of you who are leaders know what it is like when you are in front of people and the congregation are not 'coming with you'.

They're just not responding. It is hard work. And if you are not a leader who is up front, then encourage that leader who is. Be responsive to leadership. It doesn't cost anything. However, there is a dimension of leadership that most preachers know all about. There are times when the vibrancy and the anointing are missing in the meeting and you have to start from scratch. But you are a person under God, a person who is anointed, and you begin to minister in that anointing. Such is the gift of leadership.

Home group leaders among you can encourage the people to be responsive. If there is lethargy in your church, don't blame anybody else but your leaders. If there is apathy in your church, look to the leaders. If there is criticism in the church, look to the leaders. The people will mirror that which the leadership sets before them. Leaders will feed through to the people various spirits and attitudes. I am thrilled at the way my triplets – who are not saints – respond to God even at their young age. If there is a worship tape playing they will be dancing round the room and lifting up their hands and they will be singing and clapping. They even manage to do it with 'Songs of Praise' on the T.V.! You will say, 'They are only copying what they see in you.' Yes. But there are other things that they could copy. What are your kids picking up from you? What are your people in your home groups picking up from you, because they will catch that sense of dissatisfaction and that spirit of criticism. Enthusiasm also breeds enthusiasm. What is sown in the hearts of people will be reaped. Leadership that is faithless also breeds faithlessness.

When you are in front of the people in a leadership capacity you have an awesome responsibility in how you respond and react. What do you do if something happens during the meeting and you are not quite sure what to make of it? You look to the pastor or to the leaders to see what their reaction is and you adopt the same attitude. The reactions of a pastor I know are transparent. If something happens about which he feels heavy his head goes down – and so everybody else's head goes down. People will respond to that measure of leadership. If you are on the platform as a pastor, elder, deacon, home group leader or any position of leadership, people will look to you and will say, 'That is the way leadership responds.' Some people may have a desire in their hearts to be leaders and so might say, 'If that is the way a leader responds, I had better learn to respond that way also.' So it can work both ways, it can work for good and it can work for ill. You can bring a heaviness onto the meeting simply because you are standing there and not entering into praise or worship. Respond to the leadership. Encourage them.

I learned on a visit to Australia the three E's. One was the pursuit of *Excellence*, another was the *Energy* they exuded in God and the other was a sense of *Encouragement* that came through.

Don't some people read the notices well? We appreciate them. Then let's say so. That is not just back-slapping if the spirit in which we show our appreciation is that of encouragement.

People will always rise to that level of encouragement. They will also fall to that level of discouragement. If you are for ever exercising the ministry of a Fire Brigade people will eventually say, 'I will not get up because every time I do I get a soaking!'

We need to give the people the privilege to fail. God isn't so put out by things as we are. We often imagine that when certain things happen God is rushing around Heaven in an absolute frenzied panic: 'I don't know what to do. There was a fourth tongues message this morning. What do I do?' God is not put out. God is bigger than our puny imaginations. He works outside the sight-lines of our blinkered vision. He is seated in the Heavenlies. He is laughing in derision at His enemies. That's my God. Who is yours?

An environment of encouragement is a great thing. Nurture it. Don't lose it. But be responsive also, not just to the leadership but to the movings of the Holy Spirit. God is wanting worship that comes out of a desire to respond to His presence.

If there is a difference between praise and worship, it is, I believe, that praise can actually create an environment for the presence of God. Yes, God is there. God is present because 'God Is'. But there is that special manifestation of His presence where His glory fills the place. That is a level of praise that God inhabits. It is the praise of warfare. We need to respond to His presence.

I love the story of Mary before Jesus. Maybe Martha had just got used to Jesus being in Bethany. But not Mary. Mary could remember the time that Jesus came to Bethany when the smell of death was on the place. Mary could remember that where there was death Jesus brought life. Mary did not allow herself to forget. Sometimes we have grown accustomed to His presence. We no longer respond to Him; we have taken Him for granted.

Maybe you need to get out that alabaster box, that which will really cost something. It won't just be a matter of pouring out the contents and replacing the box on the shelf because it is a nice box and because it would be a nice memento of the occasion. Mary was prepared to do it as though it were for the last time. She wasn't hanging on to it for a keepsake afterwards. She wanted it to be a total expression of love.

Men, do you perhaps find it hard to pay that cost of emotion because, after all, you are a man? We need to learn to break the alabaster box and pour some of that emotion on the feet of Jesus.

The Spirit of God wants to reach those parts which nothing else can reach. You love God with all your heart, but have you put a barrier up? Have you got some 'nevers'? You might have, from a child, been taught to bottle-up your emotions, taught that boys don't cry, boys don't show emotion, taught to 'be a man'. I want to encourage you to be a worshipper. Begin to learn to pay that cost and say:

> Lord, touch my heart just once again,
> Fill me anew with wonder;
> The wonder of your love so free,
> The wonder that it included me,
> That I am now yours eternally,
> Fill me anew with wonder.

(C. A. Bowater 1985)

There might be some other area in which you find

difficulty in responding to the Lord. God isn't wanting technicians in worship. He's wanting responders, those who will respond to His presence. I don't know how you will respond to Him. I don't know how you need to respond to Him. But be responsive to His Spirit.

The world is waiting for prophetic worship. It awaits a people whose worship and daily lives demonstrate the reality of God's presence. My prayer is that God will teach us, help us and lead us: that He will bring into our lives the reality of His presence: that our lives will be real manifest-ations of the truths about Him: that wherever we go there will be a fragrance about us because we are saturated in His presence: that we will live lives of reality and be relevant to the society we live in – in our homes, in our place of work: that we might be a prophetic people bringing the 'now word' of the Lord to this generation.

My prayer is that God will not only hear our words but scan our hearts that He might see that desire to bless Him, to surround His throne with blessing, that He might see our love for Jesus and a thankful hearts full of adoration and gratitude and worship.

Jesus, I worship you,
Worship, honour and adore your lovely name
Jesus I worship you
Lord of Lords and King of Kings
I worship you
From a thankful heart, I sing
I worship you.

(C. A. Bowater 1982)

83

PART III

Discovering the Potential of Your Priesthood

Introduction

Church musicians are vital contributors to the atmosphere experienced at services. If they get it right, technically and spiritually, they will almost surely help to bring the congregation into blessing. If they get it wrong, at best they will be an embarrassment, worse still, an obstruction to the spiritual flow of the gathering.

We are seeing an extraordinary proliferation of musicians actively participating even in the most liturgy-based services. In what was once the domain of the organ alone, guitars, drums, woodwind, string and brass, percussion and all kinds of electronic gadgetry are now commonplace in many worship and praise celebrations.

Musicians, as you serve the body of Christ and minister to the Lord on your instruments, may I encourage you to extend the boundaries of known abilities and enter into the fullness of your potential – the potential of your priesthood.

The Purpose of Instruments

1. 'Sing for joy to God our strength: shout aloud to the God of Jacob!

Begin the music, strike the tambourine, play the melodious harp and lyre.' (Ps. 81:1–2, N.I.V.)

The most obvious purpose for instruments is to accompany singing, to provide melodic, harmonic and rhythmic support to hymns, praise and worship songs. It's vital for the instruments to make the songs 'feel' right in respect of pitch, volume and tempo. The art of accompaniment is an advanced skill. Accompaniments must never dominate, but can direct. To provide appropriate and differing timbre according to the style and message of the song is a vital consideration.

2. 'He appointed some of the Levites to minister before the ark of the Lord, to make petition, to give thanks, and to praise the Lord, the God of Israel . . . and Benaiah and Johaziel the priests were to blow the trumpets regularly before the ark of the covenant of God.' (1 Chron. 16:4,6 N.I.V.)

Amidst other duties the Levites, priestly musicians, were appointed by David to surround the ark of the Lord continually with thanksgiving and praise, in song and on the instruments. On their instruments they ministered to God in His presence. God must love music. The psalmist exhorts us to 'come before Him with joyful songs' (Ps. 100:2 N.I.V.), and frequently implores, 'sing to the Lord a new song' (Ps. 96:1 N.I.V.).

How limiting it would be if our involvement as musicians was merely to accompany singing. We minister to the Lord directly, we serve Him as we play. Therefore make every note intonated, every harmony completed, every rhythm created and melody weaved a meaningful, worshipful act of service to the Lord. That, as we will see later, implies greater care and preparation in what we do.

3. 'Praise the Lord with the harp; make music to Him on the ten stringed lyre.' (Ps. 33:2 N.I.V.)

The playing of instruments must be an extension of a praising instrumentalist. A player with a worshipful heart can create worshipful music. We must first of all be praising people – worshippers first, instrumentalists second. That's why God entrusted to the priestly tribe, the Levites, the awesome responsibility of surrounding His presence with music. They could handle it. Their priorities were right.

4. 'Elisha said " . . . now bring me a harpist". While the harpist was playing, the hand of the Lord came upon Elisha, and he said "This is what the Lord says . . ." ' (2 Kings 3:15–16 N.I.V.)

So many times I have experienced that Holy Spirit anointing upon instrumentalists where, from that platform of inspiration, the word of the Lord, the prophetic utterance, has been brought to the people of God. The instruments prepared the people for prophecy. Music has inherent power – it can stir or soothe the spirit, it can inspire or incite, bring deliverance or destruction. Under the anointing of God the Holy Spirit it can lay bare and prepare the heart to receive the word of the Lord.

5. They ' . . . prophesied, using the harp in thanking and praising the Lord.' (1 Chron. 25:3 N.I.V.)

'I will turn my ear to a proverb, with harp I will expound my riddle.' (Ps. 49:4 N.I.V.)

How about the thought that as well as the playing of instruments preparing the people for prophecy, the instruments can in fact be played in a prophetic manner themselves? Given that the instruments are extensions of the players, the music an expression of their hearts, should it therefore be impossible to believe that the prophetic spirit can be stirred within the heart of the instrumentalists who declare it in the way they know best, through the music? I would imagine that most of us have at some time listened to music, symphony, sonata or whatever and confessed that it had spoken volumes to us. We actually attribute speech, words, thoughts to something that is without lyrics. The music spoke to us. Sometimes, music can touch on those areas of emotions, dreams and aspiration that no amount of words could express. I believe in prophetic playing. None the less there may be times when it is necessary to clothe the melody with understanding.

6. 'Make two trumpets . . . use them for calling the community together . . .' (Num. 10:2 N.I.V.)

The instruments should call the people together and lead them in worship. Remember, it was the Levites, those who lived and moved in the dimension of their priestly calling, who were the instrumentalists. They did not play before they were prepared in heart and spirit. Truly they could lead – they had got themselves ready! In truth that cannot always be said about most of our congregations. They arrive and stumble into church in varying stages of readiness and willingness to worship and praise the Lord. The musicians should be ready, if their calling is true, to lead the people in the journey of praise into the intimacy of throne-room worship.

How profitable to the local church to have anointed and separated musicians who, as they begin to minister to the Lord, begin to draw in the people so that together they can make that ascent from things temporal to timeless worship!

7. 'When you go into battle against an enemy

who is oppressing you, sound a blast on the trumpets. Then you will be remembered by the Lord your God and rescued from your enemies.' (Num. 10:9 N.I.V.)

'Spiritual warfare' is an in-vogue subject and rightly so. Ephesians 6:12 says 'Our struggle is not against flesh and blood, but against the rulers, against the authorities, against the powers of this dark world and against the spiritual forces of evil in the heavenly realms.' (N.I.V.) The enemy of the church is not people, systems or military powers, but spiritual powers and forces. We must therefore not dissipate our energies by fighting and standing against things that are not really our enemies. If our enemy is spiritual then the resources given us by God to do combat and win victories will also be spiritual. 'The weapons we fight with are not the weapons of the world. On the contrary, they have divine power to demolish strongholds.' (2 Cor. 10:4 N.I.V.)

I recommend a book by Terry Law entitled *The Power of Praise and Worship* (Victory House Publishers). He identifies our weapons not as guns, swords, knives or the like but as rockets:

Rocket Weapon 1. The word of God: giving faith, health, new birth, light, food, cleansing and victory – in all resisting Satan.

Rocket Weapon 2. The name of Jesus: recognising that God has invested power and authority in the name of Jesus to resist the activities of Satan.

Rocket Weapon 3. The blood of the Lamb: the blood that resists the accusations of Satan, the enemy, and declares our righteousness so that we, who are made clean by His precious blood, can face the 'accuser of the brethren' and with Paul say that by the blood of Jesus, we are justified and made righteous just as if we had never sinned (Rom. 5:9), and having been redeemed, forgiven, cleansed, made righteous and sanctified (1 Cor. 6:19,20), Satan has no place in us and no power over us.

Spiritual rockets require spiritual launching pads. These include prayer, preaching, the word of testimony, praise and worship.

Terry Law says:

> When praise and worship is loosed by a group, there is a tremendous amount of power generated. Psalm 22:3 says that God inhabits the praises of His people. When we praise God together, God inhabits our praise. Because corporate praise involves the power of agreement, the power of coming into harmony, there is a tremendous spiritual energy generated. *The Power of Praise and Worship* p. 117.

Musicians, be equipped by the Spirit of God to lead the people into a dimension of praise that will make inroads into the enemy's territory. As the spirit of praise explodes amongst you, you will begin to see the fall-out of blessing and of deliverance from the enemy.

Paul and Silas prayed and sang praises to the Lord in the midst of their prison darkness, when hurt and in pain. In offering their sacrifice of praise, their prison, the stronghold, was shaken and they were set at liberty.

Has it ever occurred to you how it was that the young David had the confidence to take on the warlike Goliath? What was his training school? Did he read books on 'How to Kill Giants'? His preparation was in the hillsides as he looked after his sheep. There he got to know God, the God of all creation. He would look around at the hills, the fields, the flowers and the birds and declare, 'the earth is the Lord's and everything in it' (Ps. 24:1), he would look up at the night sky and see the moon and the stars and state, 'The heavens declare the glory of God, the skies proclaim the work of his hands.' (Ps. 19:1) Before you take on giants you need to know that the God in whom you trust is all-powerful. Not only did David develop an awesome awareness of the greatness of God, but in those many hours of solitude he developed a relationship with God: 'The Lord is my shepherd . . .' (Ps. 23:1), 'The Lord is my light and my salvation – whom shall I fear' (Ps. 27:1). Before you face giants it's necessary to have a personal walk and relationship with God. We know too, that in the course of his work, David killed a bear and a lion – God delivered them into his hands. Before you fight giants, know what it is to defeat the bears and the lions of daily experiences: habits, attitudes and desires. Unless they can be overcome the 'Goliaths' in our lives can never be defeated, but God will deliver them into our hands for us to do something about them. God will only reward us with public victories when we know victories privately.

May our worship 'in spirit and truth', and divine inhabited praise, bring many captivated hearts into liberty and release, and healing to hurting and broken hearts.

8. 'God has ascended amid shouts of joy, the Lord amid the soundings of trumpets.' (Ps. 47:5 N.I.V.)

There is a dimension of praise that God feels

sufficiently pleased with to 'inhabit'. Another paraphrase suggests that he sits enthroned in the midst of the praises. A throne is intended for a king. The praises of God's people can herald in the presence of the King. How often we sing, for instance, 'Jesus, we enthrone You, we proclaim You our King.'

The song goes on to develop the concept that He is standing amongst us, 'but as we worship we build a throne'. God does not desire to stand amongst His people, as if unwelcome or a spectator, but to reside, and to sit down on something that is appropriate to who He is. He is The King of kings and Lord of lords. He deserves a throne. Instrumentalists, know this, that the music that is required is that fit for a king. Herald in His presence. Swing wide the gates and let the King of glory come in. Let us declare His majesty, with joy, dignity, clarity and that very special unction of the Holy Spirit which transforms the ordinary into something that is mighty in God.

In 2 Chronicles 5 we read of how the people of God practised and prepared to receive the return of the ark of the Lord into Solomon's Temple. After years of floundering and mistakes, the total symbolism of the presence of God was returning to where it belonged. As the people sang and the trumpets sounded, the Bible reveals that God was so overjoyed at being welcome, that even He must have felt that He had 'come home', that He could not be confined even to the proportions of human imagination, and His glory, His manifested presence, filled the temple.

We may know very little of such an experience,

but let our spirits long and thirst for a revelation
and manifestation of the presence of our God.

> *Fill the place Lord with Your Glory*
> *At this gathering of Your own.*
> *Reign in sovereign grace and power*
> *From Your praise surrounded throne.*
> *Fill the place Lord with Your glory*
> *At this gathering of Your own.*
> *We exalt You, we adore You,*
> *Thankful hearts now join as one.*
> *You're the Christ, the King of Glory,*
> *Father's well beloved Son.*
> *Fill the place Lord with Your Glory,*
> *At this gathering of Your own.*

(C. A. Bowater 1984)

The Organisation of the Music Team

The chief musician

The chief musician has very strong scriptural foundations. He was someone who was directly account-
able to the king and had the responsibility to
choose, develop and direct the musicians and
singers in the temple services and feast days.

In David's tabernacle there were three main chief
musicians: Asaph, Heman and Jeduthan or Ethan.
We also read in 1 Chronicles 15:22 of Chenaniah
who because of his skill and his position as the head
Levite 'was in charge of the singing'.

Something about the names of these chief musicians reveals the qualities necessary for those aspiring to, or already in, such a position in the local church.

Asaph There is not an abundance of information to show us the kind of man Asaph was, other than that along with other chief musicians he was specially anointed, gifted and chosen to minister in music. There is something, however, more revealing about the man's name.

Today, little thought is given to the naming of our offspring other than, perhaps, fondly naming them after a favourite Bible character, relative or friend. There was a time when names were given because their meanings were perfectly representative of the person's appearance, occupation or personality, or merely summed up the aspiration of the parents for their child.

Asaph meant 'one that gathers together and removes reproach'. Isn't that a beautiful name?

The chief musician needs to be an Asaph. music goes beyond being just an art form. It is not neutral. It has the power to influence, damage, corrupt, destroy, bless, soothe, build up, heal and deliver. Satan is using music as a supernatural tool in these days to bind and destroy many young lives. How much more then can God, the Creator of all good things, use music as a powerful means of blessing, inspiration and fulfilment of His purposes in these last days.

There can be a great unifying work of God done through music. Every week, as your congregation comes together, from so many differing circumstances and conditions, varying in willingness and readiness to worship and praise, be an Asaph, gather the people together into one central purpose, to exalt the Lord our God. People tend to carry into church many heartaches, senses of failure, disillusionment and sorrows. They need to have their hearts and minds gently centred on the Lord and away from the place, people or programme.

As the people are gathered together and the musicians minister the anointing of God, in His presence, those with feelings of loneliness, bitterness and self-reproach can know, as it were, healing ointment being poured out into their lives. So often self-condemnationn lies like a thick cloud over people. They come in to the service and leave at the end in exactly the same state of heart and mind. They have neither been gathered together with the other worshippers or made any personal sacrifice of praise, and consequently they have not allowed themselves to be changed in His presence. The spirit of self-condemnation must be replaced with a sense of being God's child, of belonging, and the eyes that are downcast and inward-looking must be uplifted to behold the Christ, for when we behold Him, we are changed.

Gather together, remove reproach and focus hearts and minds on Jesus.

When I look into Your holiness,
When I gaze upon Your loveliness,
When all things that surround
Become shadows in the light of You.
When I've found the joy of reaching Your heart,
When my will becomes enthroned in Your love,
When all things that surround
Become shadows in the light of You,
I worship You,

I worship You.
The reason I live is to worship You.

(Author unknown)

Heman. He too was gifted and chosen, but his name meant 'one who is faithful'. Much emphasis in society today is given to spectacular, fantastic, and generally over-the-top styles of behaviour, but the essential quality required in the Kingdom of God is that of faithfulness. The ultimate benediction is 'well done, good and faithful servant' (Matt. 25:21). The final commendation is not for how skilful or ingenious we have been in the work of the Lord, but how faithful.

Faithfulness requires endurance and determination to continue, particularly when it would be the easiest thing to quit. There are times, particularly when dealing with people – specifically musicians – that frustration and exasperation can seemingly overshadow every good desire and vision. Then, qualities of faithfulness are put to the test.

Psalm 88, interestingly, is associated with Heman. It's not a psalm of glorious victory, a sense of overcoming or general well-being. It speaks of being near to death (v. 3), of being without strength (v. 4), of being forgotten (v. 5), of being separated from friends (v. 8), of being rejected (v. 8) and more! Not exactly a 'walking in faith and victory' style song! But Heman the Ezrahite was a faithful man, faithful to his calling and faithful to his God.

Jeduthan/Ethan. The name means 'one in whom is consistent or permanent praise'. Praise had become a part of his lifestyle. It wasn't switched on when the occasion demanded. It was as much a part of him as was breathing.

Have you met people like that? How beautifully infectious and influential is their spirit. They are just as exposed to the rigours and 'hassles' of life as the rest of us, but in everything, every experience, they can still return praise to God. No longer are they dictated to by circumstance or feeling. They have learned to reign in life and not lose that sense of desire continually to return to give God His due. No problem in life changes the fact that God is worthy to receive all honour and praise. Jeduthan did not live a yo-yo spiritual existence – in giving praise to God, he was consistent.

Fundamentally, I believe that praise is caught and not taught. Principles can be imparted but that sense of heart adoration can only be ignited by the Holy Spirit of praise within us.

Often, as I have travelled to different areas of the U.K. with my musicians and singers, I have seen congregations change from icy indifference, abject apathy, to real enthused expression of praise. That they were merely being stirred up could be a valid criticism. God, however, is in the business of stirring up spirits. Haggai 1:14 says, 'The Lord stirred up the spirit of Zerubbabel' (cf. also 1 Chron. 5:26; 2 Chron. 36:22). Surely, God in us would desire us to encourage, exhort and motivate His people into an expression of praise: 'it is fitting for the upright to praise Him' (Ps. 33:1 N.I.V.), 'how pleasant and fitting to praise Him' (Ps. 147:1 N.I.V.).

Chenaniah. This name means 'one who is established by Jehovah'. Do not desire, seek, or even remain in the position of chief musician if you do not have unshakeable confidence in the certainty of your calling. At best you will be a square peg in a round hole, but more important you must discover that place and function in the body of Christ that is meant specifically for you. Furthermore, by being the wrong person fulfilling the chief musician's role, you are hindering the right man or woman from entering into their God-ordained ministry. Perhaps, even more seriously, by being the wrong person in this key position you could in fact be an obstruction to the clear flow of the Holy Ghost amongst the people in your fellowship.

Give careful consideration to these issues. They may save you many years of frustrated ministry. The Church of Jesus Christ has been littered over the years with the debris of well-intentioned people, pastors, teachers, evangelists and the like, ill-equipped misfits, frustrating the workings of God. Chenaniah had an inner security that was not based on what other people thought about him, or even on a recognition of his obvious skills, but on the fact that he was established, called and equipped by God.

Practical Implications

Realistically, the chief musician must have:
Good grounding in the word of God. It is not sufficient to be super-abundant in natural skills, knowing all there is to know about harmony and counterpoint, compositional techniques, arranging skills and performance credibility. But the chief musician does need to be fully established in scriptural principles, not necessarily a theologian, but well conversant with the Scriptures.
Leadership qualities. If you are to lead, people will have to want to follow. There must be a strength of character manifesting itself in communication

skills, faithfulness, ability to exercise authority and to behave at all times with compassion. Musicians can often be temperamental, frequently over-sensitive and, generally speaking, hard to handle.

Organisation ability. In many growing churches the quality of musical activities can be mind-blowing: choice for different ages, worship groups, gospel rock groups, soloists, teams of musicians, productions involving drama and dance, recording sessions, video recordings, theory classes, instrumental tuition, travelling ministry and maybe more. All these are a normal part of the musical life in my church. There are also the services to minister at, of course! The organisation and co-ordination in itself can be a full-time job without the added desire actually to be creative in the writing of original material. By the way, the philosophy held by many, that it is only necessary to 'rely on the Lord', or wait for the 'moving of the Spirit', holds little credibility. Planning and organisation does not have to be divorced from the need to wait on God and know the Holy Spirit's guidance. They are compatible. Most people operate with more security if they know in advance when and where they are needed. Do not take your musicians or singers for granted. Plan ahead and communicate your plans precisely. However, do not become bound up with a legalistic spirit but make allowances for the unexpected!

A prayerful love for the ministry and musicians. If you try to function without prayer, it is like a car being run without oil. Inevitably the crunch comes. Friction arises, something blows up, and the whole thing becomes non-functional. Every step and decision must be exposed to the oil of prayer.

Every person in your care needs your prayers.

The musicians too are having to struggle with their own emotions, perhaps senses of inadequacy, and of course they have to cope with you!

A love for the congregation. You are a servant. To minister is to serve. Our service for God stems best from a love relationship with God and with God's people.

I was recently meditating on the Scripture in Ephesians 4:15 in which Paul implores the people, 'to speak the truth in love . . .'. Have you ever been on the end of an 'I love you, but . . .' statement? Usually the 'but' covers a multitude, dare I suggest, of sins! As I considered the verse, I began to recognise that the only environment in which truth is secure is that of 'being in love'. A couple 'in love' can share truths, maybe about each other, without a sense of being under attack and without the need to become defensive. In that environment of love for each other it is understood that the well-being of the other person is the main priority.

Chief musician, you must 'fall in love' with your congregation. You may not always feel that love reciprocated, or feel appreciated, but your love for them has got to be without measure or favour.

Does that remind you of someone? Of course. As we become more like Jesus we will love as He loved. His compassion will become ours. His priorities will find a central place in our hearts.

Choosing and appointing musicians

Pray for the musicians you need. I had the privilege in 1984 of visiting Australia and, in particular, the New Life Centre in Sydney. This church has seen phenomenal numerical growth in the six or seven year period of existence under its pastor, Frank Houston. He recalls that in the early days of his church he had received very clear direction from the Lord that music, or more specifically, worship and praise, was to be a key for future development. He began to pray that God would 'send in' the right person to head up the music in the church. The more that he prayed, the harder the heavens seemed to become. He could not understand how it was that, having been given this secret by God, the answer to his prayer was so delayed. By spiritual revelation, he realised that he wasn't getting an answer because he wasn't asking the right question. It was something like the time when God said to Moses, 'what have you got in your hand?' (Ex. 4:2). God was wanting to show to Moses that he already had the resources 'at hand' to be a man of authority under the power of God, as long as he was prepared to surrender even those things that humanly speaking appear to be insignificant.

As God revealed to Frank Houston these principles, to his alarm God also identified the answer to the prayer, a young man already in the fellowship. Trevor King at that time was a recently converted ex-drug addict hippie. The long hair, casual clothing and 'laid back' attitudes were still a part of his lifestyle. After much argument with God, Pastor Houston eventually, almost reluctantly, agreed to approach Trevor. In asking him to play at the next Sunday service, Frank inwardly prayed that the long hair might be cut, the shorts replaced by normal trousers and the open sandals by shoes. At that Sunday service, to his pastor's horror, Trevor appeared in his usual non-conformist clothes but, as he started to play, the anointing of God the Holy Spirit became evident.

Trevor King eventually became full-time Director of Music, founding with Frank Houston a creative ministry centre *par excellence*, and is now a pastor in his own right.

'What have you got in your hand?' Only a pianist, maybe a guitarist, nothing terribly significant. Pray for them, pray with them and release them to the Holy Ghost. Encourage other latent gifts and talents within the church. I have often known people who gave up their involvement in music as soon as they became Christians, thinking that perhaps it might cause unnecessary problems in their new way of life. Stir up these hidden abilities, expose them to the potential of the anointing of the Holy Spirit.

Taking lessons. Encourage younger musicians in the church to be involved in Junior Groups. I have initiated a system amongst my own musicians where senior instrumentalists coach and develop the younger people. There is an excellent principle here of giving and encouragement which I believe God can bless.

Do not expose your very young musicians to playing in the main services, even out of a desire for involvement or boosting the size of the band it is a mistake for two reasons. Inexperience can promote discouragement, and frequent discouragement can lead to youngsters with potential giving up unnecessarily. Also, playing for worship is not merely an activity, an extension of a hobby. It is a spiritual ministry. As with all ministries, together with the pleasures there are the responsibilities. It is not fair to let young musicians, who are often spiritually immature, face such responsibilities.

Maintaining standards. I was delighted when a number of my front line musicians asked for advice regarding taking private lessons. They all wanted to be 'stretched' technically so that they could be more effective in their playing. This was obviously going to be an investment of time and money and, for some, real sacrifices had to be made. It is very easy to become musically stale and even a brief series of lessons can help to 'freshen up' attitudes and understanding.

However high the standard of performance is, it is without real merit if it is not matched spiritually. In choosing musicians, who are exposed to the possible dangers of pride and jealousy and so much more, consideration of their spiritual maturity and consistency is altogether valid.

Establishing ministries. Pray for and with each musician, individually. Seek always the blessing of the Holy Spirit upon each of your instrumentalists. Make sure of their calling. It is essential that they are not misplaced in their ministry. Constantly cover them with prayer, that they might become established and rooted in God in such a way that there can blossom something that will have fruit for the glory of God.

The hurt of not being asked to be part of the music team is not as great as the hurt of being asked to step down from that position. Be careful with the appointment of musicians.

Practise together regularly

Pray together as a team. Not the hurried 'God bless us!' prayer, but lingering times of waiting on God and praying for and with each other. Many of us 'hide' behind our instruments. Our involvement covers up a multitude of hurts and anxieties. In fact, in church life in general, a role or a position held can be used as a convenient mask. Musicians must learn to pray as well as play. There is a great unifying quality in prayer. That environment of being open before God, honest and forthright with Him in front of colleagues, is spiritually healthy. One learns more about people from hearing them pray than from hearing them play their instruments.

Honesty and commitment. Musicians are very defensive creatures, especially if ability or musical interpretation is brought into question. However, if a level of gracious honesty does not exist between the team, real progress will not be made, either spiritually or musically. The know-it-all and got-it-all and done-it-all syndrome is deadly for the team relationship. It's a cul-de-sac from which there is no going on. Note that I use the words 'gracious honesty'. My experience has been that all truth has not always been clothed in love. Truth, taken out of that setting of being 'in love' is not always edifying. We must certainly be open to the truth – about our playing, attitude, reliability, and so on.

Commitment is one of the current 'in words'. But really there is no air of mystery surrounding it. Commitment is faithfulness – faithfulness to God and to His people, to the vision of the church and its outworking. Where there is love there should be commitment. What are the implications?

We need to be committed to each other's spiritual growth, development and success. A competitive spirit is not conducive to making progress in committed relationships. Commitment is all to do with relationships. When the marriage vows are taken, the promise is made to stand by each other 'in sickness or in health . . . for better or worse . . .' and so forth. There is no opting out of real commitment just because times may become hard. I have a poster on the wall of my office, showing a baboon neck-high in mud. With large penetrating eyes he implicates everyone that looks at him and says, 'We're all in this together!' There are no exclusion clauses in commitment.

I will stand by my musicians publicly and privately. There may be things that I don't like. Certain attitudes may need to be corrected, but I will always show them complete loyalty. I expect that loyalty to be returned and shown amongst the whole team.

Have a goal. If you aim at nothing, you'll probably hit it! For a practice to disintegrate into a free-for-all 'jam session' is perhaps the most common of all side-tracks. Know where you are going. Have a goal for your rehearsals. It may be to learn a new song. To teach a song with confidence takes time – time to be sure of the lyrics, tempo and arrangement. When it comes to teaching the song to your church your confidence (or lack of it) will be conveyed and mirrored. The aim of the rehearsal may be to conquer difficult keys or new chords or to prepare a 'special' for the Sunday night service.

Whatever, always have a goal. Be disciplined and you'll be more productive.

Insist on punctuality. If the practice is scheduled to start at 8.00 p.m. be there on time. No, not 7.59, but in enough time to set up and prepare so that the real rehearsal can begin at 8.00 p.m. There are some people who can always be relied on to be late. Without being legalistic, if anything is worth doing, then let it be done properly. Time is easily lost and wasted through indiscipline. It's been my experience that the one who is always late to the practice is usually a principal player, and consequently the main thrust of the rehearsal cannot begin until that person has arrived. Patience is stretched, and frustrations rise amongst those who scheduled their day to be there on time.

Establishing priorities. It's been my observation that the committed musicians can be amongst the busiest members of the fellowship. This may induce certain stresses and pressures that must be recognised and relieved. The establishing of priorities is paramount. This may be taken for granted but needs restating: the first priority is a personal relationship with God – for from this alone can any blessing flow. A first hand, relevant and refreshing relationship with God must be established in the lives of all who seek to minister. Anything less will produce mechanical, lifeless service. Musicians, be sure of your calling and discover more of the heart and mind of the One who called you!

Vitally important, too, is the keeping of good relationships within the family. Do not neglect family responsibilities. It's been said often that God made families before He made the Church. How often, though, do we see even Christian families suffering neglect because a father or mother is taken up with 'the Lord's work'. My desire is that my kids are not 'switched-off' because my involvement in ministry robs them of a Dad around the place. I want to be a good father. I want them to see just how exciting life is, how great it is to live in the revealed will of God. I want them to love life, to love God and serve Him with a full heart. In it all, I am the 'priest' in my home. I have a responsibility to love and serve my wife even as Jesus loved and served the Church. There is no credit if in the midst of all my 'serving the Lord' I actually fail to give my wife love, time and attention. We now try, with some success, to write into the weekly schedule a family time and a time for being together. If communication on a domestic level falls apart, everything else will become meaningless.

Young musicians too, honour your parents. Treat them with love and respect. I believe in having good, strong family relationships as the foundation for ministry.

If you are involved in secular employment, make sure your testimony is clear and strong. Don't be one thing at work and something else in the church. Let your ministry flow out of a lifestyle that honours God.

Take care of your health. Be sensible. Over-tiredness can so easily lead to sickness. If you're ill it's hard to fulfil your musical responsibilities. You could be letting down a pastor who relies heavily on you. Our bodies are the temples of the Holy Spirit and need to be treated with care and respect.

Do not commit yourself to a ministry that consistently won't be fulfilled. Be aware of the cost of time factors involved. Keep yourself and your ministry in correct perspective to life. We need to be complete people, separated to the purposes of God but living life to the full. We must be visual aids of what it means to have 'abundant life'. With regard to other interests: clean, healthy pursuits are vital if we are truly to relate and communicate with society today. Let us not be known for what we don't do but for what we are!

Strive always for excellence. Most of us settle for something below that of which we are capable. Do not avoid playing in the key of E^b major simply because you find it difficult. Certain songs are written in that key because it is the one best suited to its mood and melody. You can rob a song of its intrinsic qualities by transposing it simply for convenience into E major. If the theory of music baffles you, ask God to give you understanding. If playing 'by ear' is a mystery, ask God to give abilities. Whatever the situation, work hard at improving technique. Give yourself whole-heartedly to the task.

At the service

Arrive early – not just in time for the pre-service prayer meeting but before it – to tune up your instrument and make sure the musicians' area is tidy. I hate having to step over trumpet cases, bags and coats, music stands and the like – some that I have seen have been like a military obstacle course. When you're ready, don't mess about. Remember, folks are arriving at church and don't need the atmosphere of several impromptu recitals. Join the prayer meeting. You've tuned your instruments, now get tuned in yourself. Pray and worship together with the other musicians (who have also arrived early!).

Position instruments so that there is a good sense of ensemble. There must be visual contact with the chief musician and maybe also with the pastor. Watchfulness and alertness are essential. Many of our charismatic-type times of praise and worship have so much variety, making eye contact vital. I have known musicians who have not only kept their eyes closed but seemingly have blocked their ears also. I once knew a lead guitarist who would frequently get lost in wonder, love and oblivion. He would plough right on through prayers and the like. I eventually 'pulled the plug' on him. Even then there was a fraction of a moment when he didn't even know the difference!

Don't play all the time. It's not a race where we all start together and try to finish as close to each other as possible. Sometimes a song will be best served by leaving out certain instruments. Listen to each other. Sense the tapestry of sound as instruments weave in and out of the texture. Sense the movement of the Spirit of God. Enhance the song with the qualities your instrument can bring. Don't destroy the atmosphere.

Take time out from playing. Put your instrument down and get involved in the praise and worship. Your playing must be an extension of your praising. Technical proficiency is not sufficient. You need to be a worshipper first, a musician next. If your own personal walk with God is faltering, have the courage to stand down from musical involvement. Take time when you can be ministered to instead of always giving out. You cannot minister out of spiritual dryness. Become refreshed in God, then with renewed joy serve the Lord with your playing.

Provide continuity – musically and spiritually. There are times when the musicians can underscore, for instance, the reading of the word of God – out of which can flow a relevant song. An instrument played gently during spoken links can preserve the flow and spirits of a service, but this must be done sensitively and must never dominate.

Pitch and tempo. are two contributing factors to a chorus or hymn 'working'. The pitch of the song must be comfortable for the large majority of the congregation: too high and most people will give up, too low and the song will lack impetus, drive and penetration. Carefully selected modulation from verse to verse can in fact enhance a song and help to bring a sense of climax.

Tempo also is frequently not considered. Sometimes we settle for a mid-tempo feel for most of the songs which tends to produce a mid-tempo level of praise. Excitement often needs to be injected for the song to become genuinely 'up-tempo'. There are some worship songs that become more intense, more personal if the tempo is really slowed down. Certain choruses and hymns with real 'growth potential' lend themselves to multi-tempo treatment.

Simplicity. While it's great to learn all the beautiful augmented, diminished, major seventh and ninth chords, there are times when simplicity is of the essence. Genius is doing the simple things well. Congregations that like to sing in harmony can be easily confused and discouraged by musicians heavy into chord experimentation. Our motivation is not to be obscure or 'clever' but supportive of meaningful, fulfilling worship.

Begin and conclude the songs tidily. A clear, well-thought-out introduction can assist confident singing. There is no need to stop and give the starting note each time as if to say 'On your marks, get set, Go!'. Learn to create introductions that provide the correct impetus for songs, and when the song is finished, let the music clearly suggest the drawing of it to a close. Introductions and endings require plenty of rehearsal.

Bless the people with your servant's heart. Allow God to minister through you to them. Don't isolate yourself or only meet with those who can talk about music. Be an encourager of the folk. You have an immeasurable privilege in serving them. Serve them joyfully. Don't grouse or moan, murmur or backbite. Reject the 'no one understands us' syndrome that obsesses many young musicians. Seek always to play under the anointing of the Holy Spirit. It's difficult to define. It's not always easy to know 'what it is' but it is very easy to recognise 'what it isn't'!

Selah. Musicians, pause for a moment. Consider all that God is saying to you. Think on His claims for your life and ministry. Remember, first and foremost, it's not your ability that God is after – but your availability. Just as the musicians were considered a treasure in the courts of the kings of Israel, and the rich, so the Lord will consider you a treasure in His house as you minister Him.

The Singer and the Song

Singers, by the very nature of their inherent skill, are frequently over-rated in their own eyes and, in the eyes of others, under-rehearsed. The human voice needs to be gently coerced, shaped and developed. Lose your voice and you've lost your ministry. However, this finely balanced area of 'good voice' and 'good spirit' is vital.

Singers – dare to take a good look at yourself and allow God to make you into a 'vessel of honour' (2 Tim. 2:21).

Singing to the Lord involves our whole being: our spirits, our emotions and will, and our intellect. But the most important ingredient is our spirit. 'God is Spirit, and those who worship Him must worship in spirit and truth' (Jn. 4:24). Secular music is performed to impress or to move others emotionally. God's music goes beyond that, because it ministers life and truth by presenting and glorifying Jesus. This can only be done when the singers, the instrumentalists, the instruments themselves and the songs, are anointed – that is, saturated in God's Holy Spirit. Without the presence of the Holy Spirit in our lives and ministry we have nothing to offer except mere words and pretty music. But when we are anointed, and the presence of the Holy Spirit is upon our instruments and voices, we minister according to what is God's desire and will for a particular service. It is not talent that breaks the yoke over people's lives and sets the captives free but, as Jesus said, 'The Spirit of the Lord is upon me, because He has anointed me to . . .' (Lk. 4:18–19). The same Spirit that was upon Jesus is capable of radically revolutionising our ministry, causing us to serve with power and authority.

The Spirit of the Lord,
The Sovereign Lord, is on me
Because He has anointed me
To preach Good News to the poor.

And He has called on me
To bind up all the broken hearts,
To minister release
To every captivated soul . . .

Proclaiming Jesus, only Jesus,
Jesus, Saviour, Healer and Baptiser,
The Mighty King,
The Victor and Deliverer,
He is Lord . . .

(C. A. Bowater 1985)

The singer and the spirit

'Out of the abundance of the heart, the mouth speaks' . . . and sings (Mt. 12:34).
Prepare your heart through prayer. There is no short cut to knowing blessing on your ministry.

Oh, ye who sigh and languish
And mourn your lack of power,
Hear ye this gentle whisper:
'Could ye not watch one hour?'
For fruitfulness and blessing
There is no royal road;

The power for holy service
Is intercourse with God.

(Author unknown.
From: *No Easy Road* by Dick Eastman,
Baker Book House)

God is looking for those with dedicated hearts, willing to work at prayer. The word of God declares 'The effectual fervent prayer of a righteous man availeth much' (Jas. 5:16) or, to put it another way, 'the one who is in good relationship with God and gives himself to prayer . . . will see much accomplished.' Perhaps we don't see a lot happening spiritually through our ministries because we don't truly apply ourselves to prayer.

Teach me,
Teach me how to touch Your throne,
Teach me how to bring Heaven down,
To release Your power
Teach me,
The wonders of the secret place,
Teach me,
Teach me how to pray.

Teach me,
Teach me how to touch Your heart,
Teach me what it means to have faith
That can mountains move.
Teach me,
How even I can seek Your face,
Teach me,
Teach me how to pray.

Prayers of the righteous man availeth much,

And righteousness exalts a nation,
Come Holy fire of God and sanctify,
To intercede for Restoration.

Where shall we turn?
Turn to the Lord!
How shall we cry?
Cry with all our hearts.

My soul shall wait on Thee
O Lord, my God,
From Thee alone
Comes our salvation.
O God, be merciful,
Turn not away,
Let saving health
Flow through the nation.

('Teach me how to pray' C. A. Bowater 1984)

The preparation must begin with: Praying for forgiveness of sin: 'If we confess our sins, he is faithful and just and will forgive us our sins and purify us from all unrighteousness' (1 Jn. 1:9).

Sin allowed to linger in the life wrecks all real usefulness for God. It will rob us of joy and potential power. For us to be effective in serving God, sin must be removed. The psalmist said, 'If I regard iniquity in my heart, the Lord will not hear me.' (Ps. 66:18) Unconfessed sin automatically blocks the ears of God. Humble prayer and confession: 'be merciful to me a sinner', in an instant releases a flood of forgiveness (Lk. 18:13).

Prayer defeats Satan. His accusations and innuendoes are stifled as he is presented with the blood of our Lord Jesus Christ that makes us clean from every sin. (1 Jn. 1:7) See also Revelation 12:11: 'They overcame him by the blood of the Lamb'. Forgiveness removes Satan's finger-hold on our lives.

'Prayer, real prayer, intelligent prayer, it is that routs Satan's demons for it routs their chief. David killed the lion and bear in the secret forests before he faced the giant in the open.' (S. D. Gordon *Quiet Talks on Prayer*, Grosset and Dunlop, New York)

Pray for God's anointing – each time you sing. Without the anointing we can do nothing, we are nothing (Jn. 15:5). It is only the Spirit of God flowing through us that will genuinely effect lives. Many can be impressed, stirred, even emotionally moved by fine singing, but it's the Holy Spirit's working in us that actually changes people: 'Ye shall receive power after that the Holy Ghost is come upon you . . .' (Acts 1:8). God is ready to extend this power to those who will pray (Acts 2:17,18).

We can so easily plough on 'working for the Lord', relying on fleshly energy, ideas and ideals. It is not service or work that is required, but fruit. What is the 'fruit' of your ministry? 'He that abideth in me and I in him the same beareth much fruit, for without me ye can do nothing' (Jn. 15:5). See also Zechariah 4:6: 'Not by might nor by power but by my Spirit.'

If the ministry in song is clearly recognised and is not seen as simply a 'programme filler', it will then come into line with the criteria for all ministry. Christian work, whatever the manner of extending Christ's Kingdom, inevitably means a collision with opposing forces. We keep forgetting that, 'we wrestle not against flesh and blood but against principalities and powers . . . the rulers of darkness of this world . . . spiritual wickedness in high places.' (Eph. 6:12) We get nowhere until these are overthrown. Religious pomp often provides a hiding place for dark spirits. Mere preaching or fine singing will not remove them. Only an openness to the Holy Spirit, an aligning with the throne of God, and a realisation as to our true position in Christ, will bring effectiveness against our enemy. Furthermore, we need not and cannot expect to see Holy Ghost manifestation if our lives are not continually saturated by His power. We cannot live how we like and still expect God to reveal His power (Jas. 4:7).

Come Holy Spirit, come just as You will,
Softly and gently as breezes so still.
Come as a rushing wind, mighty in power,
Come Holy Spirit, come now.

Come Holy Spirit, as flames from the fire,
Cleanse me, empower me, my being inspire.
Come as the healing oil liberally poured,
Come Holy Spirit, come now.

Come as a torrent, as waves on the sea,
Sweeping away all that would hinder me.
Come as refreshment, as streams from the
hills,
Come Holy Spirit, come now.

Come Holy Spirit, come just as You will,
Work in and through me, Your purpose fulfil.
Make me much more like my Saviour, I pray,
Come Holy Spirit, come now.

Cause me to live as a child of the King,
One from whom worship and praise freely
spring,
Bring Holy Spirit revival to me,
Come Holy Spirit, come now.

                                (C. A. Bowater 1982)

Evaluate your motives. Keith Green has said:

> What we idolise, we ourselves desire to become
> with our whole heart. A lot of people want to be
> just like their favourite gospel singer and
> performer, and they seek after it with the same
> fervour that the Lord demands we seek after
> Him. We insult the Spirit of Grace to make a
> place for ourselves rather than a place for Jesus.

The Bible says, 'as a man thinketh in his heart . . .
so he is.' (Prov. 22:7, A.V.)

As a youngster, I never fully understood why it
was that my Dad would put such emphasis on the
importance of motives. Just about every week he
would warn his congregation about guarding
motives. Enlightenment must come with age, and
now more than ever I see this area of our lives as a
key. The carnal life seeks to make a reputation,
preserve and project it. The Christ-like attitude is
to make ourselves 'of no reputation'.

It is essential to die to self-made ambitions and
goals. Singer, know what it is to be dead! This is
not an excuse for false humility. 'I'm really nothing
very special,' can sound very humble and spiritual.
The true test is to see the reaction when someone
else tells the same person, 'You're really nothing
very special'! One learns most about people by their

120

reactions and not by their actions. Paul said, 'I am crucified with Christ . . .' (Gal. 2:20). In every respect the 'I' in our lives must be crucified. What 'I' am, what 'I' think, what 'I' want to do and so forth. The 'I' is central to sin and therefore to separation from the purposes of God. The 'I' must be crucified and must only know resurrection in the life of Christ. Without His life, 'I' am nothing.

What I am speaking about is not a sporadic experience; it must become a part of our lifestyles. We need daily to learn to deny ourselves (Lk. 9:23). Following Jesus demands a day-by-day, moment-by-moment willingness to be identified with His cross if we are to know Easter fruits in our ministries.

When people die they forgo any rights on life, rights of reply or bargaining rights, and they are buried. The chapter on this life is closed. The problem often, in spiritual terms, is that we claim to be dead but refuse to be buried. There needs to be a death and burial of all that is represented by the 'old life', if we are to 'bring forth the fruits' of Christ's new, indwelling life (Jn. 12:24–25).

We may as well delete the verse in Scripture which declares that, 'Old things have passed away . . . all things have become new' (2 Cor. 5:17) if we are not prepared for it to be worked out in our own lives. The truth of the word of God must, if it is to be powerful in our lives, not only be acquired but applied. Let's be radical and actually do what He says.

Hands up all those of you who have never been asked, 'What's your ministry?' Not many, I imagine. Have you noticed that when they say 'ministry', it's said as if there were some mystical quality attached to it. I must confess to becoming a little weary of the 'My Ministry' syndrome. It is time to take the capital 'M' out of ministry.

Don't get me wrong. I do not for one moment disregard the importance of finding a place in the body of Christ. I reckon though, that I know a few who have found theirs – they're 'pains in the neck'! Praise God for His giftings to the Church, but the 'Super-Star' image is inappropriate to those whose true desire is to minister. 'Let this mind be in you, which was also in Christ Jesus who made Himself of no reputation, and took on him the form of a servant . . . humbled Himself, and became obedient unto death,' (Phil. 2:5–8). So, you have a ministry? Then be like Jesus, become a servant. To minister is to serve.

Firstly, surrender that inflated ego. Singers, be honest now. How much time, either consciously or subconsciously, do you spend feeding off people's reaction to what you do. We all like and need encouragement. There should be more of it around. However, ultimately, it could become a very self-centred exercise and lead to a self-gratifying existence. What we are is more important than what we do. A reputation is what other people think about us. Character is what we really are. That's why Jesus made Himself of no reputation. It didn't really matter what people thought about Him. He knew who He was. If you have the potential to minister, it need not be supported by boastful claims. What you are will be recognised by those with the ability to 'see'.

Secondly, be a servant. Jesus took upon Himself the form of a servant. This concept is so contrary to the in-vogue claim that we, the Christian population, are going to 'take over the world'. Sure, I believe were 'in training for reigning', as John Phillips would put it. Certainly those who are 'in Christ' are seated with Him at the place of real authority (Eph. 2:6). The conquest, however, will not be by authoritarian, dictatorial methods but through servanthood. The spirit of the Kingdom of God is that of a servant. Then God will cause those who serve to be exalted, but exaltation must not be confined by our narrow thinking.

To minister is to serve. No promise of glamour or frills. Simply serve. Those who seek to minister will, by necessity, develop a lifestyle of service and let that spirit of servanthood be proven (1 Tim. 3:10). Servants will have a deep awareness of their responsibilities and a particular regard for authority. A servant will always come under authority To serve is to have a submissive spirit. 'Lone Ranger' ministries are not a part of the Kingdom of God. See Matthew 20:26–28.

Thirdly, there is a need for separation. The call to holiness is as pertinent today as it ever was. 'You shall be holy, for I the Lord your God am holy' (Lev. 19:2). There is a need for separation from the trends and standards of this age. We are to be an alternative people – a holy nation set aside for God's glory.

You shall be unto Me
A Kingdom of Priests
An holy nation
Set aside for My glory,
Hear my words and obey,
Keep my covenants every day,

You're my chosen special treasure,
Mine alone . . .
> (C. A. Bowater, 1985, from Ex. 19:5,6)

Maybe you have sung, 'Fill this place, Lord, with Your Glory'. You and I are the temples of the Holy Spirit, and His glory can only fill that which is anointed and separated to His purposes (1 Cor. 6:19).

Finally, let those of us who seek to minister, to serve, be steadfast. 1 Corinthians 15:58: ' . . . stand firm. Let nothing move you. Always give yourselves fully to the work of the Lord, because you know that your labour in the Lord is not in vain.' Faithfulness is a prerequisite. It's no good having a servant who cannot be relied upon. It appears that the musicians referred to so often in Chronicles had a set time to minister. They fulfilled their calling faithfully, stood at the posts, played when, how and for as long as they were required. Faithfulness is one of the most overlooked virtues in the lives of Christians today.

The world should know what God is saying, because the Church is living and saying it. We should see that in all areas of our lives, wherever we are, we are steadfast in all that we do.

So you have a ministry? You're a servant of Jesus Christ and His body? Then let us 'wait on our ministering' (Rom. 12:7). Let us humble ourselves before God, in awe that He should ever choose to work through us. Let's be more like Jesus.

Study and meditate on the word of God. Colossians 3:16 beautifully shows how the abundance of song will emerge from the richness of God's word in our lives: 'Let the word of Christ dwell in you richly as you teach and admonish one another with all wisdom, and as you sing psalms, hymns and spiritual songs with gratitude in your hearts to God.'

The word of God provides perspective. It keeps us in our rightful place and puts God firmly in His, as the one who is 'seated in the heavenlies', laughing in derision at His enemies (Ps. 2). The word of God is penetrating, causing motives and intentions to be truly evaluated. It is powerful, sharper than a 'double-edged sword' (Heb. 4:12)

Your Word, O Lord,
Is truth unchanged, unchanging,
A constant firm foundation,
So steadfast and secure.
All that there is written
Remains, and ever shall be.
Life itself shall fade away.
Your Word alone endures.

Your Word, O Lord,
Directs in paths of righteousness.
Lamp and radiant Light,
The way is clear to see.
Word of God, instruct Your people
And in our hearts be hidden,
Planted there, Lord let it bring forth
Fruit, abundantly.

Your Word, O Lord,
Is healing to the nations.
Your Word reproves, corrects
And ministers peace.
Lord, cause us to turn once more
To the precepts You have given,

To the life-imparting words
Of pardon and release.

Your Word O Lord
Is full of penetrating power,
Piercing even the parts
That sin would cause not to yield.
Living, energising Word, now
Activate Your people.
Revolutionise our living
And in our hearts be sealed.

(C. A. Bowater 1984)

Dealing with two enemies: jealousy and pride

Jealousy robs you of your God-given goals and gives you bitterness of soul. Without wishing to offend, my experience has been that singers are prone to jealousy more than most. I think it's because the human voice is considered to be inseparable from the person – unlike with instrumentalists. Implied criticism becomes much more of a personal issue. Therefore the interrelationships between singers are prone to more personal problems.

Realise that jealousy comes from the devil. Such an attitude of heart 'is earthly, unspiritual, of the devil' (Jas. 3:5), and where it exists ' . . . you find disorder and every evil practice' (Jas. 3:16). That's pretty clear, isn't it? The devil, Lucifer, is the author of confusion. He's an expert on jealousy.

The name Lucifer means 'light bearer' or 'daystar'. It also means 'the anointed cherub that covereth'(Ezek. 28:14). Lucifer had been given a special, distinctive commission from God, different from that of the other archangels, Michael and

Gabriel. Lucifer was the anointed cherub who covered the glory of God. He had a special anointing from God for ministering to God and covering the glory of God with music. Before 'the fall', Lucifer led the angelic host in praise and worship to the Father.

However, sin entered the picture. Isaiah 14:13,14 describes how it happened: Lucifer took his eyes off God and onto his own beauty and brilliance. He became filled with jealousy and pride. He began to desire worship for himself instead of being willing to give worship to God. As a result, Lucifer gained one-third of the angels and they were cast out of heaven because of their rebellion.

Jealousy is rooted in Satan. Guard against it. Reject it. Desire success for your brother and sister, encourage them, prefer them to yourself, do 'the Kingdom thing'. Romans 12:10: 'Be devoted to one another in brotherly love. Honour one another above yourselves.'

Keep your eyes on your own attitude and standards; don't keep comparing yourself with others in a negative way (Gal. 6:3,4); strive for excellence in ability and spirit. By all means learn from those with greater gifting and desire equal measure, but let your desires be without spite or bitterness – let them be holy desires. Always acknowledge the giftings of others and be prepared to consider them as better than youself (Phil. 2:3). Refuse to be drawn into the competitive spirit of the age. Don't let striving become sin.

Whole church fellowships can be devastated if jealousies are allowed to run rampant. Learn, and let the truth go deep into your spirit, that what you are right now, is only because of the grace of God;

and so it is with your brother and sister in Christ. And that grace is sufficient (2 Cor. 12:8).

Pride will blind you to the truth. You are deceived if you think of youself more highly than you should (Gal. 6:3).

Pride does not survive the scrutiny of the throne of God. We cannot enter deeper into God until all 'flesh-life' has disappeared. The knife of the cross must be applied as never before. Our availability to God is not based on the principle that He would be at desperation point if it wasn't for us. He probably experiences more desperation because of us. Our service, our availability, is not on our terms, but on His. Singers, we must be wholly available, to be used, or not to be used. If you can't cope with that, don't sing a lie, 'Here I am, wholly available . . .'. Availability in the spirit of servanthood means that when God beckons, we move; when He doesn't, we stay. It's a hard lesson to learn. Often we think we have learnt it then someone gets selected in our place and we find all the old feelings of rejection, hurt, bitterness, jealousy and pride resurfacing. Folks, it's time for another funeral service. The remedy can only be repentance, humility and developing a teachable heart.

'If we confess our sin . . . He will forgive us . . .' (1 Jn. 1:9).

'Humble yourself before the Lord and He will lift you up.' (Jas. 4:10)

'Clothe yourselves with humility towards one another . . .' (1 Pet. 5:5).

' . . . act justly and love mercy and walk humbly with your God.' (Mic. 6:8)

How to handle applause

It's a funny thing. That outrageous ego that makes a person dare to stand on a platform and say 'listen to me' has to be crucified, it has to be dead and buried, but then still be able to stand up in front of people with a selfless motivation.

Applause can be hard to handle. How many of you have been totally at a loss to know what to do when a congregation has broken into spontaneous applause? What do you do? Smile out of embarrassment, bow, look bewildered? Don't be afraid of applause. Rather, receive it as though gathering praise offerings to the Lord. Deflect applause that is offered to you, as a thank offering to God. Maybe you can join in and with the congregation offer your own thanks to the Lord.

At the end of the day, be sure to offer an evening sacrifice to the Lord, blessing Him for all that He has enabled you to do. Give Him the glory, recognising that it is only what He has done in you that has enabled Him to work through you.

Maybe you have been lost for words when someone has come and thanked you for a song that you have sung. It has perhaps ministered in a real way into their lives and they want to convey gratitude. Always receive these compliments graciously. It's good that people can feel free to say 'thank you'. Encouragement never hurts anyone. It's when we allow all the well-intended encouragement and compliments to change our perspective of ourselves that things can begin to go wrong. Anything that gets out of its true perspective can become sin. It has been said of secular entertainers that problems begin when they begin to believe their own press releases.

Keep in mind at all times that we are what we are only by the grace of God (1 Cor. 1:26–31). As soon as we start taking too much credit for giftings and abilities, that's when any anointing leaves us. We may impress and influence many with the natural ability that we possess, people may pass remarks on the quality of our voice, diction, breath control, sincerity, but none of even these desirable attributes will actually cause a life to be transformed. Ultimately it's 'not by might nor by power, but by my Spirit' (Zech. 4:6). Take the ministry in song seriously – but don't take yourself too seriously. It's good to strive for perfection, but there will be times when you will make mistakes, times when you'll want the floor to open up so that you can just disappear, times when you'll not want to face anyone, times when you'll feel a fool.

How to overcome stage fright

I can remember the very first time that I sang a solo in front of a congregation. My voice had only recently broken and I had delusions of grandeur. George Beverley Shea could now stand aside – the voice that was to melt a million hearts was to be launched.

The rehearsals were fine. They always are! But when the time came to stand up, my legs turned to jelly. There suddenly seemed to be a million miles of communication between my brains and my legs. I tripped up the steps on to the platform. I looked up at the congregation and whatever was causing my legs to malfunction now began to affect my eyes

– the people literally seemed to be enveloped in a blurring mist. The organist began the introduction and gave me the starting note. By now my ears had caught the dreaded disease; was this the song that we had rehearsed? I must have conveyed my dilemma by the blankness of my expression. We had a second, a third and a fourth go at the introduction. In sheer panic during the fourth introduction, I stepped out into the unknown. By the third line of the song, after a series of squeaked notes, wrong words and variable pitch, I managed to 'home in' on a close resemblance to the tune.

I still get nervous, but nerves and stage fright are vastly different. Nerves can be a useful way of getting the adrenalin pumping. Stage fright destroys.

The best remedy for stage fright is to place your confidence firmly in the Lord. Without fail I always say to the Lord, 'Lord, without your help I can do nothing, I am nothing'. Confession of need is a great starting point. God never lets down those who are prepared really to rely on Him.

'The Lord is my light and my salvation – whom shall I fear? The Lord is the stronghold of my life – of whom shall I be afraid?' (Ps. 27:1).

'When I am afraid, I will trust in you . . . in God I trust; I will not be afraid. What can man do to me?' (Ps. 56:3,11).

'Dear friends, if our hearts do not condemn us, we have confidence before God and receive from Him anything we ask, because we obey His commands and do what pleases Him.'(1 Jn. 3:21,21)

Be God-conscious and not people-conscious. What is the true source of our motivation? Whom are we singing for? For people yes, but more realistically for God. We must want to please Him first by our attitudes and desires. 'So we make it our goal to please Him' (2 Cor. 5:9). We are going to be answerable ultimately to God for what we do in His name. The day will come when every motive will be clearly seen for what it is.

Be prepared

Along with every spiritual preparation there must be a practical application. Time, energy, effort and prayer must go into our ministries; any calling must be substantiated by work. James 2:17: faith without works is dead; work without faith is useless. Any real ministry will find its proof in our full commitment to it.

'Do your best to present yourself to God as one approved, a workman who does not need to be ashamed . . .' (2 Tim. 2:15). There is more to singing a song than might be immediately apparent.

1. The choice of material is determined by the occasion, by the listener and not the least by your own abilities. Great care should be taken over the choice of songs. If more than one or two songs are to be sung in sequence then the question of balance has to be considered. Experience alone will teach how this is done.

2. The accompaniment will either enhance or ruin your song. The relationship with your accompanist is vital (whether it's a single pianist or an instrumental group). They need to be involved in all stages of preparation, including prayer, and fully appreciated for the way they serve the more 'up front' ministries.

132

3. Don't necessarily sing the song in the original key. That key may not suit your voice. Discover 'the right' key for each song.
4. 'Practice makes . . .' Well, let us at least strive for perfection! Take time to get each song thoroughly learned. Find out the places in the song where there are problems of pitch or phrasing, diction or delivery. Memorise the songs. Using a book can become an unnecessary prop. It may even become a distraction for the audience if not handled correctly.
5. Always be natural. There is no greater 'turn off' than someone who is, to use an in-vogue expression, 'a poseur'. Be yourself. Look and feel comfortable. Don't be forever apologising to the people; if a song is worth singing it doesn't need apologies. Be careful that you don't talk too much between songs. Your gifting is singing – don't detract from it with links that are too lengthy. If a song has to have a great build-up or explanation then perhaps it's not that good a song.
6. Always be flexible enough to change a song or the order of songs if prompted by the Holy Spirit, either before the meeting or on the platform.

I am so blessed with the singers God has placed in Lincoln. Flexibility is not an easy lesson to learn, but it sometimes means we have to be adaptable enough *not* to sing – in spite of all the planning. Sometimes the Spirit of God will move during a meeting making the ministry in song totally surplus to requirement. My singers have learned what it is to 'lay aside' their ministry as God requires. It sometimes involves changes of plans. Here, the singers now know that all plans are 'God willing!' Some people cannot cope with this. They have to have written details and plans in triplicate. Flexibility is the only way in a Holy Ghost-led environment. You can only truly be flexible when you are truly fully prepared.

The song writer

'Dear Chris, The Lord has given me this song. I wonder if you could tell me what you think of it . . .'

Apart from the problem of passing an opinion on what 'the Lord has given', more and more these days there seems to be a blossoming of song-writers who are looking for some guidance and direction. My files at the moment are bursting with new material sent to me, from old and young, each reflecting a freshness but also revealing a measure of frustration – what to do with this new flow of creativity.

As I looked through the pages of manuscript recently I began to reflect on my own development as a song-writer, and particularly with God's dealings in my life.

My first effort as a writer were inflicted on children! When I was fifteen I would spend weeks of the school holidays helping on beach missions on the Lincolnshire coast (this was years before the Lord led me to live in the county). To think of some of the things that I did to piano accordions in those days! But how the children sang! In fine weather and more often, not-so-fine, the gospel was sown into many young hearts. Here God first challenged me. He showed me the potential of spiritual truth, clothed in an easy-to-remember tune, in the hearts and lives of young people. The children would take these songs into their homes and many letters confirmed the impact that they made.

Opus 1 No. 1 was a gentle, waltz-like tune:

Gentle Jesus, Saviour and Friend,
I will love you right to life's end
For you died on Calvary's tree
To save a sinner like me
Like me,
To save a sinner like me.

And a little later:

With my God, nothing is impossible
With my God, all things can be done.
Yes, my God can revolutionise the one
Who looks to Him
To cleanse from every sin,
Yes, my God can do it
Yes, my God will do it
For He's a good God.

During my years at the Royal College of Music in London I drifted into a 'strange land' where the songs of Zion were neither sung, played nor written. But the Lord, in His abundant mercy, rescued me and when I was at my lowest ebb, spoke into my life and graciously restored me to Himself. A very short while after my reconsecration the Lord began to give me new songs. The one at that time that was particularly special and relevant was 'Kneeling at the Cross'. The second verse says:

How could I reject such pardon
This heart though hardened
Dear Lord would yield.
Now I see my real condition
Sinful position
In Christ revealed . . .
See how agonised He suffers
His only words . . .
Lord forgive . . .
Kneeling at the Cross of Calvary
In deep contrition
I humbly bow.

Then and now that song has a special place in my heart. It was like an altar built, a reference point with God.

At the same time I wrote a chorus that I still believe to be important:

Calvary love, grow in my heart,
Calvary love, glow in my heart,
Calvary love, fill every part
Revealing Christ in me,
Revealing Christ in me.

(1976)

And so began a flow of songs that were direct products of a relationship with the Lord. Songs that expressed what God was saying and conveyed what God was doing. Songs to encourage to love and to holiness. Songs to exhort and challenge people to 'reclaim the territory'. But with the flow I also knew the frustration. Would these songs – that I believed were God-given – ever be released beyond the local fellowship. It seemed that they never would.

Then ten years ago came the move to Lincoln. Where's Lincoln? If you look on the map it seems that nowhere leads to Lincoln . . . and that's where God took us: Rachel, a very poorly two year-old; Lesley, a very pregnant wife; and me, a very ambitious school teacher. During the first twelve months we would gladly have gone back to Solihull! God, however, was beginning to reprogramme my life, to rechannel my ambitions.

The Lord began to move in the Lincoln Assembly. It manifested itself in renewed vision, a flow of love, a depth of commitment and a release in praise. Songs, too, began beautifully edifying the fellowship: 'I'm enjoying being loved by Jesus'; 'I delight greatly in the Lord': 'I confess that Jesus Christ is Lord'; 'Jesus, your love has melted my heart'. There had been a major turnabout in our attitude to songs in praise. They changed from being 'programme fillers', 'pre-meeting warm-ups', to becoming an outward expression of what God was doing in us.

It was here, almost by accident, that the songs began to be released to the Body of Christ. But in all this time of waiting, God had taught me a vital lesson. There was little merit in the songs being released in isolation, as an entity in themselves; they flowed out from a reservoir of blessing, from an atmosphere where the Spirit of God was at work. The songs were just a part of the great thing God was doing amongst us. Thus the tapes 'Abba Father', 'In the Presence of the Lord', 'Jesus Thou art Precious' and others have reached every continent. When God releases, He does it well!

PART IV

The Power of God's Presence

The Power of God's Presence

Much has been written developing the theology and principles of the restoration of the tabernacle of David, and I am not attempting to add to these. Sufficient to say that God is no longer interested in animal sacrifices, because of Christ's perfect atoning sacrifice. God's desire today is to hear the sacrifice of praise coming from the lips of His people, the Church. The voice of praise will be heard in a new way in these last days as the praise and worship of the tabernacle of David is restored to the Church, the bride of Christ.

The tabernacle of David gives us the New Covenant way of praise and worship for the New Testament Church and Church Age. David, by faith, tasted of what really belongs to us. We are the 'new creation' people of Psalm 102:18 and therefore we will experience the fullness of Zion, which is praise and worship and the power of God's presence achieving great things for us. See Acts 16:25–34, for what God's power did for Paul and Silas in prison.

David had brought back the ark of the Covenant (or the ark of God's presence) and placed it in his tabernacle on Mount Zion (1 Chron. 15:1). But as it is with so many today, many in David's time preferred to remain with the old way of worship. Whilst David and many of the people worshipped

God in great freedom before the ark in the tabernacle of David on Mount Zion, ten kilometres away at Mount Gibeon people continued to worship under the old ritualistic order in the tabernacle of Moses. But the tragedy was that God had forsaken the old tabernacle (Ps. 78:60) and chosen Mount Zion (Ps. 78:68, Ps. 132:13). The power of God's presence was at Mount Zion, not at Gibeon!

Comparison of Worship

The purpose of comparison is not to be divisive but to be decisive. Ultimately, we must come into line with that to which God has given his seal of approval. His presence is the ultimate seal of approval.

The tabernacle of David

In the tabernacle of David, worship was characterised by vibrant sound; new songs in abundance; music (1 Chron. 23:5); praise (1 Chron. 16:4); clapping (Ps. 47:1); shouting (Ps. 47:1); dancing (1 Chron. 16:29; Ps. 149, 150); lifting up of hands (Ps. 134:1; Tim. 2:8). None of these were known in the tabernacle of Moses. In the old tabernacle only the High Priest ministered before the ark, whereas in the tabernacle of David all the Levites ministered before the ark (1 Chron. 16:37). In the tabernacle of Moses there were animal sacrifices, but the tabernacle of David knew only spiritual sacrifices (Ps. 27:6, Ps. 116:17; 1 Pet. 2:3–5; Heb. 13:15). As the writer of Hebrews said, we have not come to Mount Sinai, 'but you have come to Mount Zion' (Heb. 12:22).

The Psalms give us a picture of how they praised and worshipped at the tabernacle of David (Ps. 146:1–7, 148:1–6, 149, 150). The overriding principle is this: God is enthroned on, or dwells in the praises of His people (Ps. 22:3).

The Lord inhabits the praises of His people
The Lord inhabits the praises of His people,
The presence of the Lord addeth joy
The blessings of the Lord maketh rich,
The flow of Holy Ghost anointed worship and praise
Bring release, bring release.
Hallelujah, the Lord's joy is my strength!
Hallelujah, my inheritance is sure!
Hallelujah for this liberty
In Christ I am kept free –
Hallelujah, Hallelujah – Praise the Lord!
                                    (C. A. Bowater 1981)

The people of Zion

'From Zion, perfect in beauty, God shines forth' (Ps. 50:2).

In the power of God's presence, there will be salvation, baptism in the Holy Spirit, healings, deliverance and victory! (Ps. 87:5,6; Obad. 17; Is. 12:6, 33:5,14). God is going to give his Zion people a double portion of His anointing to come against the powers of spiritual darkness. 'Be glad, O people of Zion, rejoice in the Lord your God, for He has given you a teacher for righteousness. He sends you abundant showers, both autumn and spring rains, as before.' (Joel 2:23)

Isaiah 61:6,7 tells us more of the blessings in store for the people of Zion:

> And you will be called priests of the Lord, you will be named ministers of our God. You will feed on the wealth of nations, and their riches you will boast. Instead of their shame my people will receive a double portion, and instead of disgrace they will rejoice in their inheritance; and so they will inherit a double portion in their land, and everlasting joy will be theirs.

Satan is letting loose all he can against the Church to cause it to topple over. He is trying to finish the Church, but we, as the feet, bear up the whole body!

Our forefathers had a measure of revelation but we are going to enter into the fullness of 'all the truth' (Jn. 16:13). 'The path of the righteous is like the first gleam of dawn, shining ever brighter till the full light of day.' (Prov. 4:18).

God has a glorious path for the people of Zion to tread, but we need to realise that there will be great pressures on us and that we will need to stay alert. Jesus said, 'Watch out that no one deceives you' (Mt. 24:4), and 'Watch and pray so that you will not fall into temptation,' (Mt. 26:41).

Amos brings a timely word of caution, 'Woe to you who are complacent in Zion' (Amos 6:1). The time of great blessing can also be the time of great temptation. Don't become comfortable, careless, complacent, proud or unfaithful. The study of Abiathar and Zadok, the priests during the tabernacle of David period, teach us about this.

Abiathar was faithful to David during his wilderness testings and during the rebellion of Absalom. Reliable to the end? Sadly, no. He failed to support David at the rebellion of Adonijah and consequently lost his position and forfeited his ministry (1 Kings 2:26–27, 35). Just one moment of complacency and careless unfaithfulness. That's all that was needed. Abiathur was at the place of blessing but still fell to the temptation of a momentary lapse of zeal.

Zadok, who was the priest at the tabernacle of Moses at Mount Gibeon, was elevated to priest at the tabernacle of David and the temple of Solomon. Why? Because he remained faithful to God and to God's anointed men. And so, in Ezekiel 44, there are two groups of priest mentioned. The higher group is named after faithful Zadok. They will come nearer to the Lord and stand in His presence (Ezek. 44:15).

Even David fell to temptation. He became careless amidst all the blessings of Zion (2 Sam. 11:14). He trusted in his own strength, in making a count of his fighting men (2 Sam. 24).

But, like David in his earlier days, let us remain humble, faithful to God and dependent upon God and it will be for us as it was for him, who ' . . . became more and more powerful because the Lord God Almighty was with him.' (2 Sam. 5:10)

And so: 'To Him who loves us and has freed us from our sins by his blood, and has made us to be a kingdom and priests to serve his God and Father – to Him be glory and power for ever and ever! Amen.' (Rev. 1:5.6)

Bibliography

Ministering to the Lord Roxanne Brantk, Mustard Seed Press, PO Box 1000, O'Brien, Florida 37071, USA

Let us Worship Judson Cornwall, Bridge Publishing, Inc. 50 Plainfield, New Jersey 07080, USA

Restoration – What is it? Daniel Strazor, Maranatha Christian Centre, 1077 Angus Street, Regina, Saski, Canada, 54T1Y1

The Power of Praise and Worship Terry Law, Victory House Publishing, Tulsa, Oklahoma, USA

Worship Graham Kendrick, Kingsway Publications, Eastbourne

Where Eagles Soar Jamie Buckingham, Kingsway Publications, Eastbourne

Risky Living Jamie Buckingham, Kingsway Publications, Eastbourne

No Easy Road Dick Eastman, Baker Book House, USA